A FEW YEARS
OF WRITING

A FEW YEARS OF WRITING
INTERSPERSED WITH SOME FACTS OF LIFE
ROBERT MAXWELL

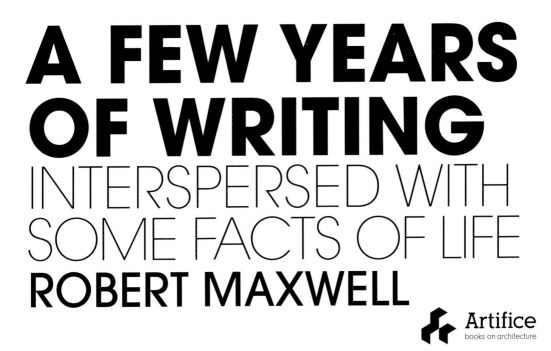

Artifice
books on architecture

For my children
Melinda, Amanda and Robert

CONTENTS

PREFACE
ANTHONY VIDLER

There are many kinds of autobiographies: the Apology, or kind that self-justifies the writer—Newman's *Apologia Pro Vita Sua* would be an originating example. There is the kind that comes clean (or apparently so)—the genre of Confession from Augustine to Rousseau; there are Memoirs that do not pretend to historical accuracy, but trace the remembered thoughts and feelings of the author in past time; more common is the self-congratulatory kind that attempts to place the writing subject into history in the best possible way; finally, there is the Intellectual autobiography that traces the thoughts of the writer in comparison with other thinkers of the time.

Architects have been especially prolific in the genre: Sullivan (who at least had the modesty to entitle it *The Autobiography of an Idea*), Ralph Adams Cram, Frank Lloyd Wright, Morris Lapidus (the last two not a little self-aggrandising), and Charlotte Perriand (who set the record, previously told by Le Corbusier, straight) would be among them. Few critics, especially of architecture have, however, attempted autobiographies. Perhaps this is a result of the need to retire behind one's subject, or simply that the life of a critic is never that interesting. But criticism itself always carries an implicit autobiographical freight—and especially so if the critic in question has been at it over a long span of time.

In this case, the architect and critic Robert Maxwell has for a long time joined practice, to teaching, to the writing of a formidable body of criticism. An earlier work, *Sweet Disorder and the Carefully Careless*, 1997, traced the author's sensibility through the period conventionally known as "postmodern", but revealed a breadth of discrimination that entirely upset any categorical imperatives of style or ideology.

The present selection of essays, written over 16 years between 1993 and 2010, brings his writing to the present and is equally revealing. But with a difference. While his friend and intellectual mentor Colin Rowe chose to intersperse his own collection of essays *As I was Saying* with autobiographical flashbacks, Maxwell calmly intercalates excerpts from the diary kept by his partner Celia Scott and himself between essays.

This juxtaposition gives rise to a number of interesting twists on the intellectual autobiography. First, the diary format gives the impression of objectivity, unencumbered by personal emotions or observations. These are kept for the critical essays. The effect is also to endow the essays themselves with an impression of statements spoken in a continuing colloquy with the architectural and artistic social circles of the period. Further, the critical essays now take on the roles of extended entries in a diary, replies to other critics, and conversations with the architects, many of whom are friends and colleagues of Maxwell.

The final result is one of complexity, density, and differentiation on many levels—rather like the layers of the Mannerist architecture beloved of the author, and in his view, the dominant trait of the postmodern period. An accomplished jazz pianist, without whose postprandial playing no dinner would be complete, Maxwell has succeeded in inventing a new genre of the architect-critic's autobiography, to intellectually enriching effect.

New York, 1 July 2012.

In what follows, RM and B stand for Robert Maxwell,
CMS and C stand for Celia Scott

1993

C receives a request from Aachen for a bust of Mies van der Rohe,
to go in the school named after him.

Dinner to Tony and Emily, George and Alessandra; they persuade
C she must do the bust, 24 January.

C, back in England, starts work on a bust of Mies, using Eduardo
Paolozzi's space at the foundry, 22 March.

B lectures on Francis Bacon at the Marlborough Gallery in NYC,
22 April.

Published: *Cinque architetture, un'idea* (Five buildings of Stirling-Wilford)
in *Casabella* 602, June.

B and C return to England and are reinstalled at Mall Studios from
1 July.

B and C are given dinner by Eduardo at the Chelsea Club, then on
to dessert and coffee at Nicole Farhi's, 12 July.

Published: *After Utopia: Rationalism from Ledoux to Ando*, in
Architecture Today, September: "the rats".

Modern Architecture after Modernism, (work by James Stirling)
in ANY, April/October.

Looked after by Cynthia Davidson, Peter Eisenman's partner, formerly
editor of *Inland Architect*.

New year's eve with Rowe and DiMaio in Kahn's Restaurant,
Westbourne Grove; Colin chats students, 31 December.

1994

B and C go on trip to Cornwall to see the Tate; give supper to
Eldred and David, 1–4 January.

Eldred has taken on board all Venturi's arguments about
communicating meaning, without seeming to realise it. B still likes
her because she liked his design for flats in Highgate.

RM publishes *Sweet Disorder and the Carefully Careless* with Princeton
Architectural Press (Kevin Lippert).

B does seminar at Polytechnic of Central London for Tanis Hinchcliffe
on the *Schröder House Puzzle*, 20 January.

Reception at the Architecture Foundation for the book signing of
Sweet Disorder, 24 January.

RM chairman for a discussion after the lecture by David Chipperfield
at the RIBA.

THREE HOUSES
TEXT FOR CHIPPERFIELD CATALOGUE, EXHIBITION IN HAMBURG

When as a young student I used to pour over the early volumes of Le Corbusier's *Oeuvre Complète*, it was not just the forms of his buildings that excited me, it was the sense that the very action of living had been renewed, that the forms of the buildings gave shape to a new life. In that first house for his parents on Lake Léman, the house and its garden came together as a machine for living, and by that token the living was made visible as never before. The fixed relationship of the garden table to the opening in the wall and to the view beyond signified a permanent hold on the essentials of life, the life of contemplation along with the ritual of bread and wine. The combined form of table and opening created a meaning: and this meaning was not just a reminder of the appropriate actions of eating and looking at the view, but the feeling that those actions, however banal in themselves, had been given a kind of final expression and raised to the level of contemplation, so that they were more meaningful than before. Something of the same excitement attends the perusal of David Chipperfield's architecture. We are given elementary forms that, in the first place, suggest their uses, and then, in a magical way, bring those uses into the realm of ritual.

These are modernist buildings, accepting the abstract forms that were invented in Europe during the 20s, making of them a vocabulary out of which a whole lifestyle may be constructed. They are also minimalist buildings, and it is possible to see now that the development of modern art throughout the course of the twentieth century has changed the perception of what minimalist forms mean, and of what minimalist architecture can attempt to encompass. Then, it was about a limitation of technique that would produce economy of construction, and the adoption of standardisation that would make available a universal method. Now, it is about renewing the act of living by cleansing the perception. Chipperfield draws this insight from within himself, but it chimes well with the discoveries made by the Japanese during the 70s, and it links to the meditative architecture of Tadao Ando during the 80s. However, it is not derived from these sources, but disposes of an innate sensibility that is the opposite of derivative.

There is no question here about the importance given to function as the basis of form, and it is clear that the architect begins by listening to his client, in order to analyse his or her functional requirements in the time-honoured modernist way. But it is also clear that each practical requirement is not accepted raw, but must first be digested in order to reduce it to essentials, to bring it to a more abstract level where it can share in the system of meaning. At that level, each action can be envisaged as being reflected within the life-system adopted by the architect. Put another way, the architect's restricted repertoire of forms requires on each occasion to be coded afresh in order to become appropriate to the actions required by the function.

If we re-examine the modern masters, we can see more clearly now that the common basis they shared in the creed of functionalism never inhibited them from staying within the range of forms produced by their own vision. Thus Corb buildings are all as much exemplars of Le Corbusier's vision as Mies van der Rohe's are of his. In retrospect, we were naive to think that the function ever was the source of the form, and was other than its instigation. A Le Corbusier building and a Mies van der Rohe building could lay equal claim to being functional, within the modernist ideology, without ever ceasing to speak of other things: in Le Corbusier's case, they were to be poetry, they were to speak to the heart. In Mies' case, they were to embody a truth about the act of building. In Chipperfield's case, they are to infuse ordinariness with a special quality: perhaps in general a sort of poetry, perhaps more specifically a sense of the moment, in order to embody a lyricism of the NOW. It is impossible to explain this architecture in purely functionalist terms, but it is equally impossible to grant it a poetic dimension without recognising in it the importance of the sense of the lived moment. If it succeeds in embodying a certain stillness, this stillness is akin to the lived moment just after attention is withdrawn, when things revert to their status of waiting, when they become mute witness to the absence of a presence.

This also makes clear why the language adopted is extremely abstract: the life movement which instigated the forms has to be reflected within a self-consistent system, one which floats, as it were, above the ordinary material of life. Put a can of Coca-Cola on one of the benches and the mood will be broken. The inmate, of course, will break the mood all the time, but clear away the garbage and the mood will return. The aesthetic is one of equivalences, not of actualities. The enjoyment sought would not emerge if the normal representational codes were allowed to reassert their all too sullied ordinariness.

As houses, all three of these buildings are machines for living, and the inmates will all the time be making them untidy, throwing dirty socks in the basket, consuming Coke. Are these interiors not altogether too precious for the ordinary moments of life? It's obvious that life cannot be lived as poetry at every moment, perhaps hardly ever, perhaps never. The same questions come to mind on looking at the interiors of Tadao Ando, where everything has been removed before the photographer's arrival in order not to compromise the vision. One remembers too Robert Venturi's polemic, where he prefers "messy vitality" over excessive order. Surely functionalism implies the primacy of function, not of form?

All these questions are undeniable, but they do not amount to a requirement that architecture be deprived of its visionary quality simply because it is intended to be lived in. To be functionally adequate is a primary duty, no more. The functional object is in the first place purely utilitarian: we do expect that roofs be waterproof, that door handles do not fall off, as a matter of expediency. But at this level, function is not yet an idea, still less a force. We are concerned here not with literal function, however essential that may be to the success of an architect, but with the expression of function as a source of idea. The actual object of use is simply used, and used up. To endow it with mental life, it has to be transcended, rendered symbolic. Then it can become the source of a vision, and of a particular vision that is concerned with the celebration of life. It is important to stress that a sense of the vitality of life is inseparable from the sense of its precariousness. This is why lyrical poetry occupies the narrow space between the acknowledgement of beauty and the recognition of its imminent eclipse. From this standpoint, a house is no less a source of extra-curricular joy than a church or a museum, and it may have an advantage in that it is dedicated to a personal existence, and shares in the precariousness of the individual life.

These houses are all designed for individuals and start from their particularity. In the case of the Knight House in Richmond, that included the need to fit into a suburban context and to incorporate the original small family house. It is characteristic of Chipperfield that this requirement has not prevented his establishing a domain of control over the whole site. The original building has supplied four walls, but it is utterly transformed by white cement render and different window openings so as to be absorbed into the new entity. The old and the new exist as two masses that complement and complete one another, and the line of division, projected at front and back, becomes a typical element of ambiguity in the definition of space, suggesting the space captured between the two masses rather than the space of frontality that divides the house from the street. The beam that straddles the total frontage, at the rear, both acknowledges this frontality and reinforces the ambiguous cut line between the two volumes. The *result* is that the spaces immediately outside the house, at front and rear, are absorbed into the internal system of the interior, become part of the play of space within the house.

The importance of capturing outdoor space within the confines of the house is evident in the Kao House, where the primary occupancy of the volume is expressed most clearly in the arrangement of the main bedroom on the top floor, separated from an open court of similar width by a glass wall. The outdoors enters as sky, not as view. From the bedroom court, a narrow stair descends in a slot to the main terrace, with its raised pool along one side. The house opens to this enclosed garden along its length, and the long window turns on to the outside wall for just a short span. Finally, on the ground floor, the house occupies the whole area of the site underneath the main terrace, and has outward-looking windows on all four sides. The house thus assures its domain of control along with its zone of privacy, before the uncertainties of the site context are known. In the House for a Collector, the openings are more liberally disposed on all fronts, but we find the same insistence on securing a domain of privacy, arranged as two levels of enclosed roof terrace, linked together in this case by a dramatic staircase ascending in one straight run. In both of these houses, the spatial order is determined *in vitro*, so to speak, before the vagaries of the site context are known.

Windows, sometimes simple punctures in the wall skin, are more often associated with horizontal slots in the volumes, running longitudinally before turning briefly on to the contiguous elevation. This system stresses solid and void as plastic entities, moulding the space with large and generous gestures, creating ambiguity with regard to scale and frontality, and dissolving any tendency to isolate elements in a way that would make them speak simply as doors or windows. This abstraction of the elements is crucial in avoiding representational links that would dissipate the vision of a special realm.

If one wants, it is possible to see many sources in this architecture. Le Corbusier is present first of all in the mode of conceptualisation, most evident in the style of the architect's sketches. These define elemental relationships between solid and void, relationships that exist as concepts in the mind and are not dependant on accuracy of drawing or a sensual simulation of the view. I used to think of Corb's buildings being fashioned out of primal material, a sort of intellectual cheese. Chipperfield defines his ideas in a similar way.

But then there are other sources that come to mind: Mies, in the importance given to changes of material, from sombre to rich, and in the use made of the right angle; Wright, in the hovering of slabs; Rietveld, in a certain neo-plastic emphasis, or maybe Schindler, in the use of interlocking forms; Scarpa, in the intensity of the planar edges; Ando, in the way that internal and external spaces are juxtaposed. This is a very reduced architecture, but it summarises the history of twentieth century architecture along the way. It is a willed architecture, controlled in order to be capable of creating its own world. It is Apollonian rather than Dionysian. It may be aware of the past, and knowledgeable about modern architecture, but not in order to stay within a zone of safety. Rather, it reviews the forms of Modernism to reflect on the meanings that were formerly passed over. It is no ragbag of influences, for everything is brought together and controlled by a consistency that is not so much logical as sacramental. There is a strong feeling for life, but in terms that suggest thankfulness rather than exuberance.

Evidently, this is to accord the architecture a distinctly Heideggerian aura; whether the author had this intention or not is another matter. We are concerned here with making an interpretation, and at least it can be acknowledged that the architecture, for all its clarity, is not explicit, and so calls for interpretation. Indeed, its appeal lies expressly in the degree to which it accepts the vulnerability of setting out to reveal an inward dimension, and to call out for a suspension of disbelief. In this respect, we are faced with a vision of some power.

THE DESIGN CENTRE IN KYOTO

It is interesting to see how the limited concerns and formal procedures adopted for the three houses discussed here, reappear in the larger framework of a public building. Built on a margin between a business zone and a residential neighbourhood, the Design Centre in Kyoto sets out to create its own internal order and to generate its own system of space. Although the main approach is recognised by a large figure fronting the street on the gable wall, made up of two strip windows one above the other, and a sort of blind, or blank panel joining them, the entrance does not go directly into the building here, but proceeds by a garden path defined by a steel fence which penetrates a lateral courtyard. It is only when deep into the site that one turns to enter near the centre. The building is made up of two interlocking volumes, as was the case with the Knight House in Richmond, and the play of these volumes creates internal views from one to the other and emphasises the autonomous spatial system desired. It is only after this system has been thoroughly articulated and controlled that the architect allows us to ascend into the roof pavilions, from which views of the mountains are no longer compromised by the huddle of roofs in the immediate vicinity.

The central staircase has a certain labyrinthine quality, it does not simply transfix the volume like an Archimedean screw, and this variety is presumably compatible with the display of different designed artefacts at the different levels. It also makes up an internal landscape where the building itself, with its handrails and its shelves, becomes part of the display. This is a landscape of precise forms balanced in a slow rhythm. Although it increasingly takes in the sky and the view as it ascends, this landscape works to exclude the ordinary world of everyday meanings and insists on a sort of remaking of the perception. Between the moment of entering the Centre, and the moment of reorienting to the mountains on the roof terrace, one has been subject to a special vision of the way space is defined and bounded. The gate on the street, the pavilions above, together make up the thread on which the experience is arranged.

In moving to the larger measure and more exposed framework of a public building, the architect has been able to reimpose his own sensibility, to slow down the consumption of space, to suggest a different time scale, to preserve his vision.

He is young, but has already achieved an architecture that does not deny the sense of life being precious, that will allow, perhaps, of the development in later projects of a more tragic sense of the human situation. In a world where life is increasingly balanced between material progress and the search for roots and identity, we need a modern architecture that can measure up to the contradictions in the human animal, one that can create depth without descending to triteness and kitsch. David Chipperfield has joined the few who have begun to show how this modern humanism may begin. It seems appropriate to stress the lyricism of its vision, one that allows both enjoyment and regret to combine, as in the words of the poet:

A lily of a day
Is fairer far in May
Although it fall and die that night
It was the plant and flower of light
In small proportions we just beauties see
And in short measures life may perfect be.

Ben Jonson: *To the Immortal Memory and Friendship of that Noble Pair,*
Sir Lucius Cary and Sir Henry Morison

London, February 1994, reprinted in Faces, Journal d'Architecture, Geneva,
spring 1994.

C's mother Eleanor moves out of Barton Close into a house designed for her by C at 33A Millington Road, 28 January.

There is builder's mess in the living room up to the last minute, so we don't get pictures of the empty space.

To IKEA with Eleanor for bookcases and bedside units, and a new desk chair, 4/5 February.

B lectures on *Architectural Education in the USA* for a symposium at Plymouth School of Architecture, 9 February.

Seminar: *Stirling with Bacon*—on 'Juxtaposition' in both—for Adrian Forty, Bartlett School, 16 February.

B goes to Lausanne for juries with Peter von Meiss, 27 February, 2 March.

B on visit to UEA with Richard Brierly to view John Miller's OPT Building, 9 March.

B gives lunch to Mark Wigley and Beatriz Colomina at Bertorelli's, 15 March.

B goes to Hamburg with David Chipperfield, gives a brief talk at the opening of his show in Aedes Gallery, 25 March.

B has lunch with Denys Lasdun at 146 Grosvenor Road, Vauxhall. 29 March.

Published: *Richard Rogers e la macchina spaziale*, in *Casabella* 611 (written in Princeton), April.

RICHARD ROGERS E LA MACCHINA SPAZIALE
TEXT FOR *CASABELLA*

Born in 1933, aged 20 in 1953, Richard Rogers is old enough to have experienced the coming of the Modern Movement, no longer as a theoretical dream, but as the practical way of implementing reconstruction after the hiatus of the Second World War. In the 30s, the Modern Movement was still an avant-garde movement, but the 50s saw it in possession of the field. Le Corbusier's Unité at Marseille was completed in 1952, Ronchamp in 1955; Mies' Farnsworth House was completed in 1950, his Lake Shore Apartments in 1951; Kahn's Yale Art Gallery in 1953. Frank Lloyd Wright was alive and well and working on his Guggenheim Museum, to be completed in 1959. Rogers himself spent his year at Yale in 1961–1962, while Paul Rudolph's new Art and Architecture Building was under construction, and his Reliance Building at Swindon, with Team 4, was completed in 1965. He is old enough then to have been immersed in Modernism from his beginning, but young enough to have inherited the mantle of Modernism, rather than to have invented it.

The great issue of the 60s, as it took over the banner of functionalism, was to evade the question of style. Modernism was a didactic doctrine, based on a deep analysis of the elements of building; it was self-consciously based on principles, and it did not want to be seen as being in any way arbitrary or subject to taste. In order to stay ahead of the critics and academics, who naturally wanted to expose its orthodoxy and reduce it to a style, it had to constantly reinvent its basis in function, to approach the real function more and more closely. This impetus accounts for what future critics were able to distinguish as a change in style—the change from the rationalist forms of the 30s to the expressionist forms of the 60s, the coming of Brutalism. Le Corbusier was a major player in this transformation, so was Kahn. Le Corbusier, despairing of finding a fine technology to implement the machine aesthetic, adopted a more earthy approach after Maisons Jaoul and Ronchamp, emphasising the sculptural aspect of construction; Kahn, with the Richards Medical Building, invented a whole new role for the services of a building, as the true mechanisms of the machine aesthetic, and incidentally, as a means of embodying a supra-human monumentalism. By these influences, Modernism was pushed closer to sculpture, and closer to the machine. Rogers' work emerges from this conjunction.

And Mies? In spite of the Expressionist undercurrents evident in his Glass Skyscraper of 1923 and his early houses in brick, he stayed close to his adopted new world idiom of pure rectangular glass enclosures, from Lake Shore through Seagram, and through the IBM and Federal Buildings in Chicago, but in Crown Hall, 1956, and again in the Neue Nationalgalerie, Berlin, 1968, he allowed the structural roof girders to be exposed as expressive elements outside the confines of the box. Structure has a gravitas that plain pipes lack. It has eschatological weight, and Mies was to the end the architect of first and last things. Throughout the Brutalist 60s, he preserved his vision of purity and danger, and remained a source of the sense of order for the second generation architects of the post-war era, and for Rogers too.

And what else? Clearly, Archigram. It was disciples of the Archigram group that, as employees of Piano and Rogers, made the design development and working drawings for the Centre Pompidou, and there is a sense in which this completed building (perhaps along with Isozaki's cybernetic environment for the Festival Plaza at Expo 70 in Osaka) is the only physical manifestation of the otherwise almost exclusively graphic universe of Archigram. But Centre Pompidou is also the building that most completely expresses the attitude to architecture of Richard Rogers. For it has no hint in it, unlike the Lloyd's building, of a conventional interior dominated by ancient tribal rituals, but is entirely the product of a free intellectual movement towards the real sources of functional truth: not only the exposure of the essential nature of construction and physical operation, the bones and guts of the building, but the devotion to the principles of change and indeterminacy in use, of which the prophet was the Archigram guru, Reyner Banham.

In one sense, with the Centre Pompidou we have at last attained that ideal of absolute truth projected by the eighteenth century theorist Carlo Lodoli, as preserved in Andrea Memmo: "Nothing shall show in a structure that does not have a definite function, or that does not derive from the strictest necessity.... No useless ornament shall be admitted.... There shall be no architecture that does not conform to the very nature of the material."[1] In another sense, we may have reached a nadir of confusion, in that reason alone does not decide that the service elements, to be accessible, must be exposed to the view, and made subject to the rigours of the weather and the demands of aesthetic appearance. Indeed, experience, which tends to follow a rather low level of common sense, has suggested that mechanical elements are best protected and hidden away, where they can be modified and maintained, and allowed to grow dirty, in secret. In the same way, the need to have every floor free of structural supports anticipates a future of adaptation that seems, in a social sense, to be both unnecessary and unlikely. It makes possible the use of whole floors as skating rinks, as arenas for fairground dodgem cars. The predominant uses proposed in the brief—as library, as art gallery—do not reasonably require column-free spaces, and the imminence of the deep structural lattices close overhead, threaded with conduits, has proved to be a disturbing ambiance for the contemplation of art works. In relation to Hannes Meyer's commandment, that architecture should be *function times economy*, this building is wildly extravagant. But in the exhibition of its private parts and in the pursuit of free space, the building only conforms to an extreme theoretical requirement that places it in a realm of pure ideology. That is even its achievement.

The exhibition of basic elements can be related to an attitude that wants above all else to avoid the accusation of suppression; that wants, as it were, to be sincere. Nothing is to be false, nothing is to be hidden away, and nothing is to be repressed. Free access to the service elements, like the creation of zones of free space, testifies to an ability to face up to the truth, to accept the consequences of pure reality. It draws attention to pipes and services in a way that parallels Duchamp's designation of a urinal as "Fountain". And it also represents a freedom from convention, a post-Freudian desire to be beyond the scope of critical analysis. It seems churlish, then, to suggest that in this free display there may be an aspect of pure exhibitionism. Is it possible that the exposed elements are there, not as necessity, but as play? That their rich pattern, epitomised in the use of bright primary colours, is a form of decoration? If this were to be admitted, it would not compromise the aesthetic effect of the building, the enjoyable feeling it promotes of being free from convention. Neither would it undermine the popularity of the building as a form of playground. But it would compromise its ideological status, its theory. For it would admit, that to achieve its decorative effect, it has poured resources into a romantic concept of architecture as decoration, and that the architect has followed a personal obsession. It would become subject to the same criticism that Robert Venturi made of Paul Rudolph's Crawford Mansions, when he compared it unfavourably with his own Guild House because the whole building had been gratuitously convoluted into a Brutalist composition of towers and grooves in the interest of expression, but in the name of necessity.[2] The architect had hidden artistic intentions behind a show of candour. Is this not the case with Pompidou?

This question lies at the heart of our attitude towards the High-Tech school, of which Rogers is perhaps the purest representative. It is not that the High-Tech architect eschews beauty. But the beauty to be uncovered has to be identified with necessity, the result of applying reason along with engineering principles. It has to exhibit an order that is not due to convention, but to nature; to be true, not to rules of human perception, but to laws of natural beauty. The architecture must be somehow protected from any hint that it is the result of a purely aesthetic intent. In engineering, it is possible to see by analysis where the engineer has departed from purest necessity in the interest of beauty, as in certain works of Calatrava. No one reproaches him, for works of engineering are usually all too brutally the result of business management and cost-benefit studies. The problem arises within architecture because its social programme prevents it from following pure engineering principles.

It arises especially in Britain, where the public concept of the architect places him into society not as an artist, but as a technological expert. For the architect to admit to artistic intent, other than as a servant of society, is considered bad form, and therefore virtually unmentionable. It is this public attitude that causes the British architect to reject any justification that is not technological in import. Even the Classical Revivalists, in Britain, rely on a justification from technology, claiming that the traditional way of building, with cornices and window sills, is a practical answer to climate and custom, and avoids uncertainty and expense. However, if it is allowed that the high cost of High-Tech buildings arises out of their quest for an unusual beauty, this does not invalidate them as a form of artistic expression. It does however put them in a theoretical bind: for artistic expression is not judged by everyday rules, nor by simple economy, but by a historical perspective within which culture evolves and cultural criticism is made. Rogers here exercises a preference which limits the cultural perspective to those aspects that he can identify with:

> The history of architecture should be seen as a history of social and technical invention and not of styles and forms. It is those periods when change quickens and turning points are reached, when innovation is more important than consolidation and the perfecting of style, that interest me most. I prefer Brunelleschi to Michelangelo....[3]

Within this perspective, however, the High-Tech is not specially privileged, but must offer itself to be judged as an expression of the avant-garde. It undertakes the purpose of avant-garde art, which is to change consciousness and prepare the future. It offers one way of criticising the status quo and of identifying with the future, not yet apparent and therefore, not yet corrupted. It aims to avoid that endless succession of forms, as defined by Georg Simmel, by which culture places itself into a historical perspective. According to Simmel, one form must replace another, since all in turn lose their power to liberate and become obstacles to new expression. In this perspective, the High-Tech response is open to criticism precisely because it holds too closely to its identity. It is an established resource applied to new circumstances rather than arising out of the attempt to define a continually changing consciousness. One can criticise recent works of Rogers as being too clearly the result of a *parti pris*. Instead of being, as claimed, a tool in the service of humanity, the method of construction becomes an artistic strategy, and hence an end in itself.

In the Tokyo Forum Project of 1991, for example, the spaces of use are first enclosed in gleaming steel shells, then supported on curved steel keels, then suspended from a metal armature, then approached by a complex of escalators. The rationale is to double the use of the expensive piece of land. By hoisting the auditoria spaces into midair the ground is freed to act as a covered plaza, in a Tokyo that is bereft of urban spaces, and that has up to now had no use for them. The resulting appearance is of an industrial installation: This would have been one of the most transparent of all Rogers' buildings, putting on show not just air-conditioning ducts and lifts but the very essence of the building. Instead of partially dissecting the elevations, there were to be no facades. Rather the building would have consisted of nothing more than an expressed structure and suspended capsules housing the auditoria. The metaphor that the Rogers team adopted to describe the scheme was that of a dry dock with three large ship hulls suspended in a protective cradle. The auditoria would have been faced with steel plates, just as though they were ocean-going liners.[4]

It is curious that, in an architecture that claims the mantle of Functionalism, the framework of metaphor is not rejected, so long as the metaphor is one that projects the character thought appropriate to industrial civilisation. Steel plates are not the most amenable materials for sheathing cultural spaces, but they become mandatory if the status of the metaphor is to be preserved. Thus, in the name of providing a service to mankind, the space of use is transformed into a complex structure and raised to a metaphoric purpose. It becomes a symbol of its own otherworldliness, a cathedral to progress.

Does this interpretation not clash with the architect's stated aims: to liberate mankind from thraldom to material slavery, and lift the spirits? Paradoxically, the expression achieved, while trying to evade the limits of materialism, reinforces them by exposing the effort required to transcend them in a purely material way. The Tokyo Forum design continues the same strategy developed in the Centre Pompidou, only extending it to a more extravagant scale. The cultural expression of the High-Tech solution is always the same, an expression of the power of material science, like a space machine, or a military project. It envisages a future where man is empowered, as if by magic, but it does not explain how mankind is to share in limited resources.

The Tokyo Forum project through its extravagance and size has a distinctly apocalyptical aura. Other works of the Rogers office in Japan are disarming by their relative smallness. The buildings for the K-One Corporation also benefit from the chaotic context in which they are situated. The question for the client in these cases is not the cost-benefit assessment of the space provided in use, but the visibility they bring to his operation. The exclusive image is all-important, whatever the expense. The most attractive is probably the least extravagant—the refurbishment at Kanda Jimbocho of an existing office building. The concrete structure is retained, and masked by a new facade of light elements, flanked by a lift tower. The result has all that one could wish for in a modern building: economy, elegance, style. The same feeling of clever design is apparent in the Roppongi Studio, with the studio for photography and fashion displays hidden in the basement, and a brief trapezoid of offices raised above. In the Tomigaya Exhibition Tower, the problem was to achieve a reasonable space of use in an area subject to severe zoning restrictions, but not to a height limit. Here, the tactics of hanging out the servant cubicles, of making the roof restaurant a tented structure, and of leaving open the basement, make up a strategy for gaining useful space within strict limits. The building becomes a single structure, a tower supporting a crane jib, from which the exhibition spaces are hung. To persuade the client, a model was constructed in Meccano, and the building proposed keeps this look of being an elegant toy.

Richard Rogers has shown himself by his writings to be sincerely concerned with the need for positive policies of social betterment, in the face, not only of the exploitative excesses of late capitalism, but of a perspective that includes increasing pollution, despoliation of the built environment, ecological disaster, poverty and population growth at a global scale. To meet these problems, he rightly calls for the application of technology and of the inventions of the most brilliant minds. Paradoxically, the clients whom his buildings best serve are those operating at the peak of the capitalist wave, those for whom image is more important than cost-benefit analysis. His desire is to push architecture as far as possible towards engineering, in order to extract the maximum of material drama. This desire brings an architecture that is optimistic in the spirit of the young officers who led the charge of the light brigade. It is marked by boyish enthusiasm.

Rogers has admitted to being greatly affected by the publication of Jane Jacobs' book *The Death and Life of Great American Cities*. He understands how the life of the city requires the mixing of uses, the overlap of structures. He points to the civic spaces of the European city as essential aids to the maintenance of a viable public realm. Yet his chosen way of building emphasises the character of industrial installations, exactly following the principles laid down in *Vers une architecture* 50 years ago. The obvious result is to identify the new facility against the rest of the city in a way that works towards its isolation, not its assimilation into the city as a whole. In this he appears to ignore the real possibilities that are now becoming visible within Modernism; the proposition that a modern building could draw its strangeness, not from its internal organisation alone, nor from its purely material conditions, but from its interpretation of the tension between internal and external forces, between the demands of the programme and those of the city, between identity and continuity.

Yet he is also a modern architect, with the instinct of starting always from the client's brief. When that brief emerges from a concern with a city region, or a city quarter, the outcome takes a rather different form, a form that acknowledges the need for continuity. We see this in his proposals for the European Court of Human Rights at Strasbourg, 1989–1994. Here the elements into which the complex is broken down are not the service elements as such, but spaces of use; they stand on the ground, forming a horizontal composition that is less obsessively analytical and more expressive of human use and intercourse. The curves are somewhat exaggerated, in a way not unlike that of Erich Mendelsohn, clearly the imposition of a strong personality; but the result seems more spontaneous, fresher, less predictable. The building takes its scale and shape from its context on the curve of a river, and from its situation within the city. The expression is no longer purely mechanical and physical, and the building gains a dimension in human meaning and appropriateness.

Rogers has many other projects under consideration in France, and there are a number that seem to open up an altogether more humane perspective, such as the masterplans for Strasbourg Étoile, 1988, Dunkirk Neptune and Port Aupec, 1990, and schemes for Bussy-Saint-Georges, 1989– and Sextius Mirabeaux, 1990. In all of these there is a distinct element of rationality and of contextual relevance. There is no compromise in the architecture, no element of kitsch or commercial opportunism. The buildings take their scale from the context, and adapt to their sites (sometimes oddly shaped) with ingenuity and imagination.

Typical of these schemes is the very elegant project for the Alcazar, in Marseille, 1988. Within a seven-storey height limit (surely a *donné* for the French city) he inserts a wedge-shaped volume closely into the texture of the adjoining blocks. Service elements are still lined up on one side, office space on the other. Between them, is a 'spine', which at ground level becomes a pedestrian route linking the frontage on the Cours Belsunce to the quiet contained space of the Place de la Providence. The way the building draws back to allow the space of this quiet square to be drawn into the scheme, the way it curves gently to make an entrance from the Cours Belsunce, show a distinct sensitivity not only to an analytical idea of urban form but even to the sense of civic propriety. These steps contribute to the uniqueness of the place without in any way compromising the idea of the architecture. Clearly, Rogers is a superb designer. Clearly, his feelings for beauty and for the traditional role of public space are sincere. We may thus hope to see his architecture come to terms, not only with the city, but with the ongoing continuum which joins civic space to cultural continuity.

At Pompidou, the structural frame behind the escalators has a classic dignity and grace, and the public place, which the building forms with the ancient city of Paris, is positive and useful. The Place Beaubourg has been as popular as the Centre Pompidou. Its shelving shape pays tribute to one of the greatest civic spaces in the world—the Campo in Siena. With that awareness, Rogers has shown himself to be capable of more than boyish enthusiasm for the Meccano set.

London, February 1994, published February 1994.

1. See De Zurko, Robert, *Origins of Functionalist Theory*, New York: Columbia University Press, 1957.

2. Venturi, Robert, "The Duck and the Decorated Shed" in *Learning from Las Vegas*, MIT Press, 1972, 1977.

3. Rogers, Richard, *Architecture—a Modern View*, London: Thames & Hudson, 1990.

4. Sudjic, Deyan, in "Nine Projects: Japan". *Blueprint Extra*, no. 3, 1991.

SOURCES

Rogers, Richard, "A Case for Modern Architecture", text of a lecture, London: Smallpeice Trust, Royal Society, November 1989.

Rogers, Richard, *Architecture: a Modern View*, London: Thames & Hudson, 1990.

Sudjic, Deyan, *Nine Projects: Japan*, London: Wordsearch, 1991.

Sudjic, Deyan, *Foster—Rogers—Stirling: New Directions in British Architecture*, London: Thames & Hudson, 1986.

Piano/Rogers, *Entretien avec Antoine Picon*, Paris: Centre Georges Pompidou, 1987.

Rogers/Fisher, *A New London: Based on Royal Academy Exhibition* "London as it could be", 1986, London: Penguin, 1991; *British Architecture Today,* (with texts by Fulvio Arace and others), Electa, Milan, 1991.

Slessor, Catherine, "Richard Rogers and the Modern Inheritance", *Planning* (Johannesburg) no. 25, January 1993.

Welsh, John, "Embracing Green (Rogers in Japan)", *RIBA Journal*, vol. 100, no. 9, September 1993; "Rogers in Tokyo", *Architecture Intérieur Crée*, no. 247, March/April 1992, pp. 20–21.

Pawley, Martin, "Rogers—Global Architect", *World Architecture*, no. 18, July, 1992, pp. 32–55.

Pawley, Martin, "Rogers and the twenty-first century", *A+U*, no. 5 (236), May 1990, pp. 7–22.

B and C in Easter trip to Cambridge to take photos of 33A for her brochure, 3 to 6 April.

Mandy and Barney visit 33A for drinks with Eleanor and inspect the new house, 16 April.

We take Colin Rowe to dinner with the Ikonomous in Eaton Square. Going home, B is breathalysed. 23 April.

The cops, observing C conducting a wobbly Rowe to his front door, assumed B too must be drunk.

When C asked why he was stopped, they said: "he turned right out of Gloucester Road too carefully".

Because he wasn't sure, from the shape of the junction being curved to the left, that you could turn right there.

Buy plants for Eleanor's garden and put them in, in time for her housewarming, 29 April to 1 May.

B and C in trip to Paris to see Nicolette Boillot: she gives a party for us and lunch at Maisons-Laffitte, 3 to 9 May.

RM lectures at AA for Alan Balfour, on *Ethics in Building*, followed by dinner at the Etoile, 19 May.

Evidently, Mark Cousins enjoyed the talk; the following year RM was employed as a lecturer at the AA.

B and C in trip to USA still using green cards, staying at Peacock Inn and the Princeton Club, 20 to 30 May.

B contributes to *Architecture as Art*, in *Contemporary British Architects*, Royal Academy and Prestel, NY,

B to Aberdeen, inspects Ed Jones' residential towers, writes them up for *Architecture Today*, 9/10 July.

TOURS DE FORCE
ARTICLE FOR *ARCHITECTURE TODAY*

Up north where the long evenings induce a sense of euphoria, the River Dee runs in a deep channel belted by trees. On the edge of the northern bank lies the young campus of Robert Gordon University, formerly the Robert Gordon Institute of Technology. To date the campus consists of only two large buildings, each one of which covers a lot of ground: the Scott Sutherland School of Architecture and the Gray's School of Art. The first is a 50s extension to an 1872 granite mansion; the second a Miesian rectangle of considerable distinction (Michael Shewan, 1966). Between them a grassed declivity dotted with art objects, known as the amphitheatre, provides a rolling space that separates the two extensive buildings and yet draws them together. The two buildings define the space. The scene in early June is idyllic. The architects (chosen on their record, not on a specific proposal), were asked to provide 50 study-bedrooms without spoiling the idyll.

They thus had the opportunity to study the problem in full consultation with the client, personified in the figure of Vice-Principal Gavin Ross, who in a former life had trained as an architect with Louis Kahn in Philadelphia, and could read his architects' minds without effort. A whole series of possible sitings was reviewed, including a low U-courtyard partly dug into the hillside, all looking to minimise the impact of student accommodation.

There were some suggestive precedents: Rafael Moneo at Wellesley College had preferred a compact, high building rather than to spread institutionally over a lot of ground; Tod Williams and Billie Tsien at Princeton had shoe-horned a tower into the corner of a collegiate Gothic courtyard without spoiling it. How about towers? It then transpired that building residential towers is a Scottish pastime going back to the days of defensive houses, nothing is more local in its appeal, and so the idea of towers became the preferred solution. The form happens also to coincide nicely with the tradition of grouping student rooms in sets around a staircase.

A good idea, but only an idea: it still required imagination and a will to form on the part of the architects to turn the idea into a practical reality and not only not spoil, but positively improve the campus: to deploy that in-between process that Louis Kahn characterised as the opportunity for design to correct intuition. From this process of meditation comes a whole series of crucial decisions: the decision to divide the accommodation into two, to have two towers of contrasting character, to site one romantically on the lip of the escarpment, the other more picturesquely attached to an existing building, to make use of the prime geometries of square and circle, to break the prime geometries into differentiated volumes that accentuate character and provide practical solutions, to subdivide the accommodation with only five study-bedrooms per floor, to offer the common room on the top floor as the ultimate definer of geometry, to study the planning on consecutive floors closely so that the tower geometry—square and round—does not constrain the layout, but emerges clearly only as the crowning shape, and so on.

In the result, the square tower naturally attaches itself to the corner of the architecture school, happily masking the dismal wall of the lecture theatre, and creating behind it a narrow townscape space that prefigures a day when the campus will be more dense and more urban. The round tower naturally moves out into the belt of trees on the edge of the river escarpment and looks up and down the river like an episode in a Walter Scott novel.

As to the means of construction, it was necessary to find a method that would be both economical and reasonably permanent: a good local tradition came in handy here, for rough-cast render on crumbly old stone has been used successfully in the restoration of ancient castles (Terpersie Castle is only a few miles north of Aberdeen) and could therefore be used to civilise the rough male kiss of concrete blocks. The earthy colour is also a local tradition, and has the additional virtue of identifying the new buildings as pertaining to the campus as a whole and not to the architecture school only.

Architects, more than lay people, will notice the acumen with which the service elements support the main figures, the way the elements emerge more clearly floor by floor as they rise up the side of the building, the neatness with which copings and weatherings are managed at each change of profile, the way the windows are grouped to provide figuration, the way the doubling of the windows in the round tower changes the scale and provides an echo of rationalist precision, the use of glass tops to send down light and provide orientation and so on. All that is part of the lore of design, like technique in playing an instrument. However, it appears that the locals passing down the riverside drive on the other side of the stream, have come to appreciate the glow of the glazed staircase caps as a landmark. The buildings have already entered the local myth.

This is clearly a conciliatory modern architecture, not a radically subversive one: an architecture that serves the client and contributes to the enhancement of daily lives. Is this the limit of its achievement? The smoothness with which it has been folded into the local scene is, however, deceptive. Without an understanding client, without the opportunity to explore alternatives and work closely with the local planning authority, the result could well have been resisted as intrusive and metropolitan. The exercise demonstrates again that modern architecture can continue to benefit from its original ideological aim of serving the user.

London, June 1994, published July 1994.

Frank Gehry gives the annual discourse at the Royal Academy; RM voices thanks. Then dinner, 11 June.

RIBA holds a celebration for the Gold Medal awarded to Michael and Patty Hopkins, 21 June.

We have dinner with Colin Rowe at his flat in Gloucester Avenue, with food prepared by Celia, 30 June.

RM to Moorfields Eye Hospital for cataract operation on right eye; afterwards, Dalibor Vesely brings wine, 13 July.

The operation was successful, B is still short sighted, but less so than before.

B publishes *Über Alles*, a critique of a prototype design by Michael Wilford, *RIBA Journal* for July.

ÜBER ALLES
ARTICLE FOR *RIBA JOURNAL*

We have here a design for a prototype regional depot for the STO Company, which produces building supplies, mainly self-coloured wall panels. The depot is made up of four elements: warehouse, offices, exhibition gallery and an information/training centre. The novelty of the design lies in the lively way in which separate expression has been given to each of these four elements, with the possibility that on other locations around Germany they can be rearranged to suit different contexts. The juxtapositions are sharp, clear and joyous and seem to be from the hand of Stirling, but he, alas, was gone before this attractive commission was landed, and if there are traces of the master's hand, it must be because Michael Wilford was an intimate part of it and is equal to the challenge of continuing in the same vein that he and Stirling developed together. This is hardly a matter of complaint. All of the work in which Stirling had a hand is to appear shortly in a volume from Hatje of Stuttgart. It will be a wonderfully full and comprehensive record of Stirling's production since Düsseldorf, during which time Michael Wilford was his sole partner, and no doubt will become something of a design manual for young architects. Now it looks as if there will in time be a third volume of prime material, from Wilford's hand alone. Michael Wilford is to be congratulated on cutting the formal tie with Stirling-Wilford cleanly so that henceforth attribution is not in doubt.

The Hamburg depot will be located on a corner site in a light industrial park on the fringe of the city. The warehouse occupies the bulk of the site and follows its rectangular geometry, and the other elements are set at various angles to make a scene on the corner, tied together by a curving wall that houses an exhibition gallery and loggia. The space thus enclosed is partly a deeper exhibition area and partly a garden. There is a lot of enjoyment in the way this curved space accommodates to the straight line of columns supporting the offices above, before developing its own loggia facing the garden. The circle is reinforced by clearly defined side walls, acting as radii, which allow a central reception desk to be masterfully located on axis. The angles of office block and training pavilion have been carefully worked out so that the spaces left over between them feel good. The outside structural bay at either end of the office block is simplified to a large single span arch that acts as *porte-cochère* for cars, at one end, and provides a grand face to the garden at the other. As with so many Stirling-Wilford designs, the free clash of geometries turns out to be based on a neat disposition of the functional requirements, a happy blend of freedom and informality that makes sense above all to the user of the building. There are no loose ends.

The volumes are as well developed as the plan. The vaulted roof of the office block, which contains a loft for future expansion, gives extra height to the administration area and allows it to assume a certain precedence over the warehouse. At the same time, its shape is vaguely Loosian and dignified. The integral canopy along the front of the warehouse provides shelter and a welcoming note for visitors and customers. Wall panels provide textural interest, as well as displaying the firm's products. The freestanding logo tower makes an accent to the approach road. At the rear, the styrofoam store is safely isolated and makes its own brief reference to a Stirling school of early vintage.

So this is modern architecture of the kind that Stirling practised all his life: spare, functional, but lively, with an evident enjoyment of form that responds to function with a surplus of energy. It is in the same vein as the Salford Arts Centre and the Temasek Polytechnic. Michael Wilford and James Stirling seem to have been so thoroughly assimilated to each other that the good work can continue, without the one. We can but be glad.

The nature of this commission involves the opportunity to rearrange the elements of composition to suit different sites, maybe up to ten all told, and there must be a hesitation as to whether the repetition that this will involve will diminish the effectiveness of the buildings, considered as a sequence. Can they continue to reach always the same standard of excellence? Can a management venture incorporating multiple outlets contribute to the future of architecture?

The basic problem with work of this kind is how to deal with the industrial shed. The normal British answer is to put art into the structure, which makes it challenging, but expensive. Or to revert to the long-standing tradition of well-serviced anonymity, with a deadpan construction that looks artful to the cognoscenti, dumb and ordinary to everyone else. A different answer was given by Frank Gehry, who turned his factory at Vitra into a design museum by decorating its public frontage with a sculptural play of architectural forms, never mind that the shed behind stays as dumb and ordinary as ever. The STO complex leans towards the Gehry solution, providing interest on the public faces out of a play of architectural elements, but without exactly embracing the idea of decoration as an accepted goal. It will be quite difficult to repeat this feat 30 times without diminishing the effect.

On the other hand, there have been some cases where an industrial client has acted as a patron of good architecture, the most famous being that of Olivetti during the 50s and early 60s. At that time good design was synonymous with standardisation of parts, not with variety of composition. But good design adjusts to the conditions of the time. Stirling-Wilford has already acted for Olivetti, not only in the Training Centre at

Haslemere, but in a fabulous headquarter design that remains a project. Troubled with declining sales, Olivetti has recently come back to architectural design as capable of providing a boost for their public image, and it seems that STO, like Olivetti, like Braun, appreciate the sales value of good design.

There is no doubt that Stirling was always equal to the scale of industrial architecture, sometimes conceived in grandeur, as with Siemens, sometimes with an undercurrent of Expressionism, as at Melsungen. In the present case, each building is relatively small, and destined to be tucked away on a variety of nondescript sites, on trading estates and industrial parks, sites suitable for the IKEAs of this world. Each context will be different, but the opportunities will have more to do with neatness and compactness than with affecting the general environment. At Hamburg, already, in the architect's own words, we have a largely featureless context. The chance to have an urban impact will be small. The lucky ones will be the customers, who will come upon something out of the ordinary during their ordinary pursuits.

London, June 1994, published July 1994.

RM starts teaching in the Graduate School at the AA, employed by Alan Balfour, from September.

RM contributes "Introductory Essay" to *James Stirling, Collected Works 1982–93*, Hatje, Stuttgart.

Goodbye party at Oxford for Colin Rowe, organised by David. Colin is going back to the US, 27 August.

We have a trip to Sicily: Segreste, Selinunte, Piazza Armerina, Syracuse, Taormina, Cefalu, 14/22 September.

Proceed directly to Naples where RM lectures on *Modernism and Tradition*, and joins trip to Capri and Villa Malaparte. But still we don't get inside the Malaparte.

We attend lecture by Bernard Tschumi at AA, and dinner afterwards, 10 November.

RM invited by David Mohney as member of a group in a public discussion on *The Changing Profession* for the Student Section of the AIA at the University of Kentucky, Louisville, Kentucky, 24 to 28 November.

B and C give a good party at Mall Studios, everyone enjoyed it, 8 December.

Celia's mother, Eleanor, has her first Christmas in the new house; a visit to her made memorable by hoar frost on every tree, 24/26 December.

Construction of Channel tunnel completed (site work begun 1987), end 1994.

1995

We give a party for Nicolette Boillot, and fork supper for eleven guests, at Mall Studios, 12 January.

AIA awards citation to RM's book *Sweet Disorder and the Carefully Careless*, March 1995.

We fly to USA for spring break; Celia lectures on her portrait heads at the New York Academy of Art, 4 April.

RM review of work by David Chipperfield *Journal d'architecture*, Univ. of Geneva.

THEORETICAL PRACTICE
REVIEWED FOR *BLUEPRINT*
David Chipperfield, *Artemis*, 1994

With this book, David Chipperfield has demonstrated a new potential for leadership, and for influencing the future development of architecture. Paradoxically, his message is that buildings are powerful only to the extent that they concentrate on their material limitations and create meaning out of their own internal structure. But, given that his buildings already speak powerfully for themselves, their ability to impose their own value is not vitiated by this text. His language is spare, epigraphic, didactic. It clarifies his intentions and permits us to read meaning into the forms he adopts. The book is an important supplement to an already influential practice.

It has a clear structure: in the first half, his theoretical ideas are interleaved with photographs of some of his buildings; in the second half, illustrations of unbuilt projects are interleaved with descriptive text. Buildings and unbuilt projects are impressively coherent, clearly imbued with a single vision.

These are modernist buildings, accepting the abstract forms that were invented in Europe during the 20s, making of them a vocabulary out of which a whole life-style may be constructed. They are also, in spite of their author's disclaimer, minimalist buildings. Minimalism in architecture started as a limitation of technique that would produce economy of construction, and the adoption of standardisation that would make available a universal method. Now, minimalism is about renewing the act of living by cleansing the perception. Chipperfield makes it clear that architecture in its present conditions must abandon its original ideology, indeed every attempt to impose a preordained theology upon it. Instead, it must return to its own limitations, and discover the as yet undefined values that may emerge from a strictly local knowledge. There is no question here about the importance given to function as the basis of form, but it is also clear that practical requirements must first be digested in order to reduce them to a more abstract level where they can create syntactical meaning.

If we re-examine the modern masters, we can see more clearly now that the common basis they shared in the theology of functionalism never inhibited them from developing a vision. In Chipperfield's case, the vision is about infusing ordinariness with a special quality, perhaps in general a sort of poetry, perhaps more specifically a sense of the moment, in order to embody a lyricism of the NOW. It is impossible to explain this architecture in purely functionalist terms, but it is equally impossible to grant it a poetic dimension without recognising in it the importance of the sense of the lived moment. If it succeeds in embodying a certain stillness, this stillness is akin to the lived moment just after attention is withdrawn, when things revert to their status of waiting, when they become mute witness to the absence of a presence. Evidently, this is to perceive a distinctly Heideggerian aura: the appeal lies expressly in the degree to which the architect accepts the vulnerability of setting out to reveal an inward dimension. In this respect, we are faced with a vision of some power.

In a world where life is increasingly balanced between material progress and the search for roots and identity, we need a modern architecture that can measure up to the contradictions in the human animal, one that can create depth without descending to triteness and kitsch. David Chipperfield has joined the few who have begun to show how this modern humanism may begin.

London, December 1994, published February 1995.

THE TEXAS RANGERS
REVIEW FOR *BUILDING DESIGN*

Alexander Caragonne, *The Texas Rangers:*
Notes from an Architectural Underground, MIT Press, 1995

This is a book that is sure to amuse many architects, by the deft way that it combines theory of architecture, a history of architectural education, biography, personal reminiscence, and gossip. Baldly, it relates the story of how two inexperienced European teachers—Bernhard Hoesli from Switzerland and Colin Rowe from England—came together in a provincial American school of architecture at The University of Texas in Austin, undermined its certainties, revolutionised its teaching, provoked its revenge, and left after only a few years to consolidate their own careers elsewhere.

The conjunction of these two was catalysed by the appointment in 1951 of Harwell Hamilton Harris as Director of the school. An experienced architect in Los Angeles, Harris was expected to bring new life to a school all too patently in need of fresh input. His interest in teaching was limited, and he expected to be able to combine the job with new commissions, and enlarge his reputation. He needed to have some young lions to energise the teaching and do the heavy work. He had the power to offer experimental appointments, the kind of opportunity that America has thrived upon.

Hoesli arrived in 1951 and left in 1957. Rowe arrived in 1954 and left in 1955. What they achieved together was effected in less than two years, and there is little doubt that in this brief interval they succeeded in changing the nature of architectural education in the United States and beyond. The book traces the revolution step by step and document by document. Hoesli, a methodical worker, kept copious notes and maintained an archive. Rowe, more selective and less obsessed, has a retentive memory.

Hoesli, a product of the ETH at Zurich, was conscientious, with the morality of a born teacher, anxious to explain as much as to indoctrinate. He cared about his students, wanted to lead them into understanding. The old pedagogy, a weak compound of Beaux Arts methodology and Bauhaus aspiration, could not withstand his enthusiasm, nor Harris his sincerity. Rowe was a scholar, a former student of Rudolf Wittkower at the Warburg Institute, a superb critic with a sharp eye. Intellectually, he was, simply, brilliant. It was fortuitous, but opportune, that the Director's wife, Jean Murray Bangs Harris, could not withstand Rowe's charisma.

Mrs Harris was the power behind the throne, and her need to protect Hamilton was combined with a need to protect American culture. The situation in Texas called for domination of the region, and in her eyes, the achievements of Frank Lloyd Wright in California and Arizona should be summed up and made available at Austin. Rowe was astute enough to know that European sources would be in competition with American values. It was becoming un-American to even know too much about Europe, which had slid too far towards socialistic nihilism. He was quick to seize on the Americanness of Mies in the Chicago scene. That allowed the inclusion of early Mies, whose De Stijl manner could be traced back to Wright of the Wasmuth era, hence related to Cubism, so permitting at least a mention of Le Corbusier, Rowe's principal obsession. The full delicacy of this operation, which secured the cooperation of the Director without alarming his wife, has yet to be appreciated, and waits to be clarified by the publication of the essay "Texas and Mrs Harris" in Rowe's forthcoming book from MIT.

But this story is not simply a case of personal opportunism, nor of a dreary struggle for bread between old and new guard. The two revolutionaries really had something to offer. The combination of their personalities provided the necessary momentum, but it was the combination of their ideas that changed the world. Briefly, Hoesli provided a methodological basis, from his need to offer a clear understanding of the process of design. He showed how the program could be analysed, reduced to elements, and recombined in a new way, far from the superficial imitation of accepted formats that was the most that the defunct Beaux Arts could manage. Rowe provided an intellectual framework, in which the knowledge of precedent could unexpectedly inform the new resolution. Precedent was remarkable, not for its conformity, but for the achievement it had represented in its time. At a stroke, history was brought alive, and originality was provided with incentive.

Both teachers were open to new aspects in the analysis of art, particularly the psychological underpinnings in Gestalt Theory that informed the Warburg Institute and the writings of Richard Arnheim. Now the mutual definition of figure and field allowed a new, deep appraisal of the ideas that lay behind form. Knowledge of the process of seeing, and of reading form, allowed the process of analysis to look with equal intensity at process and product. Most important, the material of architecture, that essence which could be manipulated in the name of discovery, was not the material envelope, not technology, still less mere appearance, but space.

Within a year, the new teaching took off. Hoesli sustained the enthusiasm of the students; Rowe provided unexpected insights, whether in his studio rounds, which were frequently interrupted by trips to the library (usually to consult Palladio or Letarouilly), or at the reviews of work, when he could impose unexpected readings of the students' work. An excitement was generated that would outlast both critics' brief spell at Austin. The momentum was maintained by the arrival of new teachers, whose enthusiastic acceptance of the method lent it a greater credibility, enabled it to survive the loss of Rowe. John Hejduk, Bob Slutzky, John Shaw, Lee Hodgden, Werner Seligmann, were all to distinguish themselves. It was this second wave, passing on to Cornell and Cooper Union, which gave rise to the legend of the Texas Rangers.

Alex Caragonne tells the story with wit and compassion, and an erudition that is equal to the task. The book will interest all architects who have tried to teach, but it also makes an important contribution to the history of ideas.

London, 1995, published 17 March 1995.

A CRITIC WRITES
REVIEW FOR BUILDING DESIGN

Essays by Reyner Banham, edited by Mary Banham, Paul Barker, Sutherland Lyall, Cedric Price, University of California Press, 1997

I once had occasion to evaluate Reyner Banham as a historian (in *Architectural Design* no 8/9, 1981), and came to the conclusion that he had all the respect for the facts (and the cautious concern about getting it wrong) of the well qualified art-history man. His scholarship was well founded and he was extremely well informed. He saw himself as a hands-on, observational historian, like Nikolaus Pevsner and Henry-Russell Hitchcock. One who not only checked the chronology, but visited the buildings.

How then came about his reputation for dismantling shibboleths, puncturing reputations, dispersing illusions? What price his outspokenness and irreverence, his sometimes outrageous opposition to the art and architecture establishments, his championing of Archigram and other fringe benefits, his taste for jumping the gun into the immediate future, whatever the risk?

Well, it was as a journalist that he began writing, and all these essays first appeared in a variety of journals. These essays are journalistic, each one immediate in its impact and every one fraught with its moment.

Early influences are decisive, and Banham's stance as a close observer of the world and its things, owes a lot to his first career choice, as a student in management training at the Bristol Aeroplane Company, "aeroplanes being a Banham family passion", as Mary Banham says in her notes on his career. From this initial commitment it seems reasonable to deduce his lifelong interest in serial production, light structures, high-flying technology, and accurate information. This identification with material efficiency provides him with a ground space from which to criticise the profession of architecture as a mystique, and architected buildings as unnecessarily heavy and indifferent to human comfort and impending social realities. He regretted the architected base of the Post Office Tower while praising the engineered aesthetic of its radio mast. And he loved Stirling for employing standard greenhouse glazing within the privileged Oxbridge campus.

This position allowed Banham to operate as an outsider. He could comfortably criticise his friends the architects for their absurd hankering after eternal verities and monumental expression, while staying close to their day-to-day problems and ahead of them in anticipating their general direction. Inevitably, his position was partisan: he was a natural proponent of a technological architecture, and liked the anti-monumental wherever he saw it: in Archigram, in the Smithsons, in Bucky Fuller, and in British High-Tech. He was the declared enemy of pretention in all its forms, and of the establishment wherever it was stuck-up ("the Royal toffee-nosed Automobile Club"), and he was deeply suspicious of formalism, while at the same time acknowledging the will to form, very much in the terms that Lou Kahn did, shifting it from the architect's intention to the innate purpose of the thing-in-itself. This point of view enabled him to puncture any over-inflated proposition that came his way, and to stand before the wider public as a prophet of the "immediate future".

Given that position, it is fascinating to discover that at the time of his death he was working on a book titled: *Making Architecture: the Paradoxes of High Tech.* Banham was partisan, but he was not blinded by technology. He wanted architecture to be true to its nature, but the more he thought about that, the more mysterious that became. He could see that Brutalism, as a credo, had not delivered the future he hoped for. That "topological architecture" was not inspired by a privileged principle of connectedness. He could see that weight and mass, considered from a scientific point of view, had environmental advantages. So these essays have a great virtue, not just in reviving for us the quintessential Banham whose irreverence we all enjoyed, but in charting the course of a subterranean Banham who had survived an immediate future that did not exactly follow his own prescription.

For, along with the cheeky polemicist, there was always the trained historian. The polemics tend to constitute a "rhetoric of presence", which I attributed to him and which he acknowledges in his New York Inaugural (never, alas, delivered). The trained historian looked to what the facts alone could justify. It is not that Banham trimmed his position to match the unfolding of events, it is rather that he always allowed space for confirmation and reappraisal. It is fascinating to see this space defined as early as 1960 in his essay "Stocktaking", where he allows that a true scientific history would include everything known, and never discard what was ideologically unpalatable. And where he acknowledges also that the city, which is after all the mark of a civilised society, could not be constructed without in some way crossing the boundary between tradition and technology.

The final essay, "A Black Box", is remarkable in putting forward a belief that I have always held, but would not dare to state so succinctly: that Hawksmoor had something essential that Wren had not. He makes only preliminary steps towards disclosing what that mysterious quality might be, and I am not convinced that it is entirely wrapped up, as he suggests, in the Italian Renaissance concept of *dissegna*, or that it is restricted to Western architecture of the Mediterranean basin. But, if one regrets the loss of Peter Banham it is above all to regret the loss of a thinking mind.

London, 6 March 1995, published 28 March 1997.

We fly to Florence, stay with the Petersons, RM in juries for Steven: we start with champagne in the garden; however, it rains continuously from the first evening, and everything is green, green like Ireland, 21–27 April.

We give dinner to Wilf Wang and the Ikonomous at Mall Studios, 6 May.

RM in trip to Germany to take part in Schools of Architecture conference at Weimar, 31 May to 4 June.

Lecture: *Convention and Theory in Architectural Education*, Association of European Schools of Architecture, Weimar.

We attend the Royal Academy annual discourse given by Arata Isozaki, and dinner, 10 June.

We attend the RIBA for Colin Rowe's Gold Medal. RM introduces him: *A Few Words for Colin Rowe*.

A FEW WORDS FOR COLIN ROWE
RIBA GOLD MEDAL

Mr President, Distinguished Guests, Ladies and Gentlemen:

I am honoured to have been chosen to introduce tonight's Gold Medalist, who might be thought to need no introduction. On the contrary, I think he needs a very careful introduction, above all here in Britain, which he has abandoned for a wider horizon.

In Britain, where they always check on the colour of your socks before addressing you, there has been confusion about the colour of Rowe's socks. Classicist or modernist? Icon or Guru? Polemicist or scholar? Banham managed to create a culture of the immediate future by avoiding virtually all contact with Rowe, but it's noticeable that when he did address him, he was careful and respectful. For my generation, those two were the poles of a debate and for some, the horns of a dilemma.

I asked Colin once, why settle in the United States, what was the attraction? His answer was, as usual, candid: "Robert, don't you know I am a Whig? Where else can a Whig go today?" It's true that at one time Colin's only reading seemed to be Lord Chesterfield's *Letters to his Son*. He was also word-perfect in much of Hilaire Belloc, especially the one that begins: "Lord Lundy from his earliest years/ Was far too freely moved to tears…" A few days ago he was invigorated by the news that a woman, wishing to fraternise with the lions in Washington Zoo, had climbed fences and crossed hahas, only to end up being eaten, a fate that Belloc might easily have prepared.

When I entered the Liverpool School of Architecture, in September 1940, I came to his attention (I think that is the right expression) by doing a sketch design for new housing where all the upper storeys were shunted sideways by half a house, creating a very odd effect of a sort of Viennese socialist paradise, a sort of Red Neasden. It was done out of pure naivety, but Colin saw some deeper intention in it, and when he and his circle entered the studio, I always received a call.

Not much new building was around in the war years, so we looked endlessly at books. Buildings were scrutinised in plan, section and elevation in order to see what scandal they concealed, what bounds they had transgressed. In this way, I received an architectural education. This was in spite of the current ideology in the school, which refused everything except Dudok and Mendelsohn. Subsequently, Colin was apt to attribute to me intentions that I was not aware of. In my second year he converted me to Corb, but prefers to think that it was I who imposed this dogma on him, because, he said, "Corb has given me a lot of grief."

They nearly failed me for doing Richard Meier stuff in 1942. Then Colin went in the army, and started training in the paratroopers. It was around this time that he had his first meeting with Jim Stirling, with momentous consequences for the future of British architecture. I took advantage of his absence to modify my style in the direction of Mendelsohn, and managed to pull out of trouble, but was careful not to let Colin see the results.

In one letter I received, his description of the barracks as "so long that the curvature of the earth effectively conceals the other end", seemed not merely to be hyperbole, but a careful examination of the evidence. This trend intensified after he was invalided out of the paratroopers, and a transition from architect to scholar occurred, which led to his studying with Rudolf Wittkower and entering into a sort of Palladian inheritance. Nevertheless, he never lost his sense of architecture as a unique form of mental activity: the creation of physical evidence that thought and feeling had been at work.

The insistence on seeing architecture as the intersection of thought and feeling gave his subsequent criticism an indubitably personal note, not unlike the art criticism of Adrian Stokes. Yet, without any professional PR, without ever managing his career, he conveyed possibilities that have changed the course of architecture in England and in America. The finesse that he employed in introducing Corbusier and Mies to the School at Austin Texas was not so much premeditated as precipitated by his intense sense of personal relations, his appreciation of people as the multiple sites of conjunctions of thought and feeling. No one knows more about how patrons of architecture came to seize opportunities of building.

This acute sense of the social gave Rowe's view of architecture an important freedom from standard art-historical classification. For a time, many of us believed that the Villa Stein at Garches was really commissioned by the Duchesse de Guermantes. Rowe imbued Le Corbusier with a style that he hardly deserved. By the same token, architecture of any period could be scrutinised for its potential today.

This is quite different from promoting postmodernism, and those who can't see the difference have been blinded by the zeitgeist. It is indirectly due to Rowe that many students studying for the doctorate at Princeton, and at other places, are architects by training, and approach the historical evidence with an understanding of how buildings come about. He has thus, without caring a fig for Cultural Studies, brought Architecture squarely into Culture. In the succession of Gold Medalist scholars, he supplies an antidote to Pevsner's materialism and Summerson's unnecessary capitulation to the programme as theory.

Mr President, I ask your indulgence for Colin Rowe.

Given 20 June 1995.

9H, NO. 9: ON CONTINUITY
REVIEW FOR *BUILDING DESIGN*

9H, No. 9: On Continuity, Eds Rosamund Diamond and Wilfried Wang,
9H Publications, Cambridge MA, 1995

NUMBER NINE of 9H appears after a gap of six years, so that what we have is a book rather than a magazine. The longer preparation time has resulted in a sharpening of the editors' view of architectural criticism as a genre. Unlike journalism, it is to be evaluative and moral rather than predatory and opportunistic. But this ontological status nevertheless defines a form of writing entirely secondary to the act of building. Building is a compulsive creative activity immersed in life. It can benefit from, but can dispense with, words. As an occasion for criticism, it remains the primary act.

The buildings treated in this volume are little known, sometimes marginal, and are not selected for their passing interest, but for the complex, and sometimes disturbing, issues that they raise for the act of criticism. The book aspires to a strong ideological position, a continuation of the preference for the hard line over the soft, the 9H pencil over the 6B. As with all strong positions, it lays claim to an objective view. The rejection of a merely journalistic approach has forced consideration of longer term values, and this has led to the theme of continuity, by which separate acts of building may be assessed together in a regular way, related to the social conditions of their time and associated with a philosophical system.

In their introduction, the editors point out that architecture, as a form of expression embodied in buildings, cannot be thoroughly revolutionary. Built form has a certain inertia that prevents it from following surface ideas and fashionable trends. It is not to say that architecture is too slow a dancer to be able to contribute to the movement of culture, but that its state of being embodied embeds it in a complex phenomenology.

The rate of building in itself superficially constitutes the rate of change in society; closely studied, the changes within certain aspects of any and all buildings more accurately describe society's real rate of change. The premise of this approach is that buildings, embedded as they are in use, are better evidence of the actual evolution of society and its transformation than other forms of expression, which may be freer to mirror the surface, but are less sure of touching the essence. The essays gathered together here are quite varied in their methodology. The first, by Luis Moreno García, on Lewerentz, starts from the discovery of a set of photographs taken by Lewerentz on visits to well-known sites. They are mostly studies of fragments, snatches of mosaic flooring, details of sculpture—surfaces, textures and boundaries—and the author makes a neat parallel between this fragmentary approach and Lewerentz's preference, in his own work, for detail rather than whole. In this way, Lewerentz appears as a sort of proto-postmodernist, recuperating recognisable figures, but only on condition of avoiding traditional hierarchies. The language used is elliptical and poetic, as when García illustrates a trait in Lewerentz's work by reference to one of the fragmentary photographs rather than the work itself.

Sonja Günther's biographical sketch of Lilly Reich, on the other hand, is strictly objective in its approach, simply describing the events of her life, the dates, where she worked, with whom she worked, as incontrovertible facts. Against this level background, the author's awareness of the special difficulties that Reich had to contend with as a woman pioneer of design comes over as entirely reasonable. She is able to draw a parallel between Reich's work with Mies, and Charlotte Perriand's work with Le Corbusier: in both cases the great men listened, benefited, and then took the credit.

Several of the essays deal, in considerable detail, with architects that few of us have heard of. The fascination here is to be brought to realise how much the history books have over-simplified the history of the Modern Movement.

Erich Altenhofer's account of the long drawn out restoration of the Munich Pinakothek, an important work of Leo von Klenze, is also objective in tone, and treats the story as so much local history. We are left to glimpse the fascinating moral landscape in which the subject of the essay—the architect Hans Döllgast—cast about for a magic formula. His problem was to find a method of restoration that would somehow preserve the authenticity of von Klenze's work along with the monumentality of the hole torn in the main facade by war damage. Rebuilding the gap in a simplified way might do this, preserving the trace of the war and protecting von Klenze from the indignity of being restored—that is, simulated, by a fully imitative insertion. This approach found some support because it was also cheaper. In the end, however, Döllgast's advice was almost totally ignored. But his struggle allows us to explore a certain sensibility that condenses around the act of restoration: a reluctance to displace what history has produced, and a desire to identify the zeitgeist, not as an overriding platitude, but as a point of precision. Döllgast lives only in this fragment of history, but not without advancing the cause of architecture: now we better understand Giorgio Grassi's more successful career.

Equally fascinating is Dimitri Philipides' account of the life and work of Cleon Crantonellis, an elusive figure whose architecture might pass as ugly and ordinary, were it not for the detailed examination provided here of dates and places, a history which permits us, again, to glimpse the moral landscape in which the architect approached his work. His problem was: he wanted to be modern, but he also wanted to be Greek. To be Greek meant that the work must have recognisable aspects; to be modern meant that it must be innovative and of the moment. Crantonellis struggles with this problem in the straightforward way of a practising architect, not applying ideas from books, but trying to live the double loyalty he required of himself. A certain transparency results, which allows us to see his work as an expression of the zeitgeist, there, in Athens, and nowhere else.

Perhaps the most interesting of these essays is Astrid Staufer's "On the Work of Luigi Caccia Dominioni". Born in 1913, Dominioni has lived through the whole history of the Modern Movement in Italy. His career was not very productive, and only three buildings are examined here, all in Milan. The work was not particularly influential or fashionable. What is interesting, for us, is to see how, in its cultural context, the architect has struggled with the conflicting demands of use, of style, of taste. This is revealed by the careful and minute examination of the buildings, in plan and section as well as in views. The author thus provides a documentation of the very process by which the zeitgeist is translated into action. This is not to deny the architect originality, but rather to focus on the uncertainty of that process.

The essay on "Six Key Buildings of Modern Architecture in Central Europe", is probably at the heart of this book. The re-examination in detail of these plans reinforces the individuality of each, dissipates the stereotype, and allows us to feel the vulnerability of ideas. By intensifying the examination of the evidence, the editors have redefined the process by which architecture thinks its way into the future.

London, July 1995, published 25 August 1995.

RM lectures in Medellin, Colombia, on the past and future of London.

There he attends a lecture by Jean-Louis Cohen on the past and future of Paris.

And celebrates his birthday with a cake baked by his lady hosts: all very friendly people.

Henceforth he vows to drink only Colombian coffee, 5 to 9 July.

RM contributes to *Contemporary Architects*, St James Press: a Royal Academy initiative.

RM to Berlin, where he makes a short introduction for David Chipperfield at the Aedes Gallery, 15 September.

Lecture: *The New Expressionism*, for VIII Seminario Internazionale Architettura e Città Univ. Naples, September.

B visits the Judge Institute, Cambridge (formerly Addenbrookes Hospital) by John Outram. 2 October.

RM in symposium on the *Royal Festival Hall* at C20 Society, organised by Ken Powell, 28 October.

Where Norman Engleback confirms that RM was responsible for the river facade as it is today.

We attend a grand charity dinner at the Grosvenor Hotel for Maggie Keswick, 16 November.

1996

RM lectures at the Glasgow School of Art on *Stirling*, for Gavin Stamp. 19/20 January.

We go on vacation in Florida: beach walks, pelicans, egrets, crocodiles etc., 4 to 11 April.

But along the edge of the sea, hundreds of dead fish, killed by a growth of weeds.

To Cornell for Rowe Festschrift: Princeton Club NY, Holiday Inn, New Haven, Princeton Club NY, 24 April to 1 May.

Lecture: *The Animated Archive*, for the Colin Rowe Festschrift at Cornell University, 27 April.

RM arranges to give signal to the slide operator by touching his nose; then forgets, and soon gets too many slides.

RM, while staying with Grahame Shane, hears Simon Schama lecture in New York Cathedral, 29 April.

RM publishes *The Two Way Stretch* in *Academy Editions'* "Polemic" Series, April.

RM to Dublin to inspect the Temple Bar Redevelopment: works by John Tuomey and Sheila O'Donnell.

He contributes *The City Takes Shape* to Temple Bar: the Power of an Idea, Dublin, May.

TEMPLE BAR FIVE YEARS ON
THE CITY TAKES SHAPE

It is five years since Temple Bar Properties organised a competition to find ways of restructuring the Temple Bar area. The competition produced 12 interesting entries drawn from large and small architectural studios, and it is perhaps a happy augury that it was won by a group of young architects who had combined specifically to take part in the competition, under the name of Group '91. These young architects, by their joint approach to the structure plan, created the conditions for a result that would reflect not only a common purpose, but a varied response. They were all hungry to design buildings, and young enough to seize any chance; but they shared a vision of a thoroughly modern architecture that would refresh Irish Eyes, and still generate the elements of traditional city form.

Five years on, the benefits of their accord are plain to see. The area is developing consistently and logically, but without the excessive design control that has spoiled so many recent attempts at moulding civic space. Each studio has worked to demonstrate its excellence in designing buildings, but never at the expense of taking over the common ground. The personal differences in their approaches have contributed to a lively and assorted mixture that blends easily into the street, even if it proclaims its own certainty. There is nothing themed about the result. The area retains its original character as a grid of small streets mixing historic relics and commercial accident, and the new insertions have not compromised its character or harmed its vitality. In promoting the competition and in trusting in its outcome the government has shown something like wisdom, and this is enough to make the result unusual as well as impressive. Much remains to be done, there are still unwanted spaces and decrepit remains, but it is not premature to declare a success in the making.

For the overseas critic, there is a special interest in the initiative because it seems to mark a moment in the development of Irish culture that benefits from a horizon that is plainly European rather than Anglo-Saxon. The holding of the competition coincided with the year of Dublin's designation as European City of Culture. In the very concept of proposing new buildings that at the same time define public spaces, the critic can discern a debt to certain broad ideas about continuity in the city, that stem from the Italian Aldo Rossi and the Luxembourgeois Léon Krier. European cities on the whole have been more aware of their inherited context than the new-world cities with their lust for skyscrapers and their duty to fill the void. Krier worked for a time with the English architect James Stirling, and several of the members of Group '91 learned their craft in Stirling's office. Stirling himself had a vision of a modern architecture that would never be compromised by half measures, yet would be capable of working with the existing context. Stirling was undoubtedly influenced by the architectural critic Colin Rowe, who used his observations of Italian cities—particularly Rome—to criticise the ideological nature of technological modernism, obsessed by the single building and oblivious to the city as a whole. To these influences we can perhaps add a Spanish dimension, since David Mackay, a key member of the competition Assessors, practises in Spain. The vitality of recent Spanish architecture, after the removal of Fascist constraints, has been compelling, and the way in which the city of Barcelona in particular has benefited from its role as venue for the 1992 Olympic Games has been exemplary, and exhilarating. The year 1991 was a good year for Dublin, when it achieved the status of a truly European city.

Dublin as a city is luckier than most, in the very fact that it has not been eviscerated by high-rise monsters. There are a few regrettable instances, it is true, but the city still holds together, with its Georgian and Victorian inheritance, its superb set pieces, and the peculiar scale and modest size that allowed Joyce to terminate *Ulysses* with Bloom's peripatetic philosophising across its width and breadth. It is a city that has been written about, that is impregnated with its tragic history and that resonates with the literary amplification of its events. How satisfactory then that it should now be able to demonstrate that history does not kill development, that the endemic conditions of postmodernism are not a cause for despair.

The result must depend a great deal on the policy by which Temple Bar Properties has been partly funded by the state, but given the freedom to raise private funding as well, and to pursue its aims of cultural regeneration without undue interference. A system of tax incentives has been approved, and this gives a means of drawing in new sponsors, who expect to be able to operate eventually on a fully competitive commercial basis. This initiative allows the whole venture to cut years off the normal period of waiting for values to rise. At the same time, to be able to count on government support in setting up new cultural centres has been a great advantage. And for the young architects, to be able to design for modest institutions as well as for those ventures that are immediately viable commercially, has been opportunity and challenge combined.

So we have a Film Centre, a Photographic Archive, a Multimedia Centre, a Music Centre—for pop as well as classical music—, an Applied Arts Centre, a Children's Centre, a Museum of Viking Inheritance. None of these are free-standing buildings: all of them are attached at some point to the existing city fabric. In all of these cases, the designers have taken seriously the implications of building not just in, but into, the city.

An important feature of the Group '91 structure plan was the policy of accommodating to the scale and texture of the existing city fabric. This from the beginning meant more than observing frontages and height limitations, it involved paying attention to the way buildings address and clarify existing spaces, and also mould the spaces behind them, where back land has the potential to open up to new pedestrian ways. In addition, there has been a will to make new spaces appropriate to the quarter: an entirely new street joining two adjacent streets, to improve east-west permeability, for example; and more conspicuously, the transformation of empty sites previously used as car parks to create new squares. In the case of Temple Bar Square, we find a new mixed-use and residential development that looks south across the whole north side of the square, defining it as an enlargement of Temple Bar, the main east-west route, and incidentally creating a sort of skateboard forum, a place for junior to hang out, for mothers to gossip. In the case of Meeting House Square, all four of its sides have been reinforced by new buildings, all by different hands, all different. An auditorium opens into this space for open air performances, and films will be projected from one side of the space to the other. It is more of a room than a street. This amounts to a revitalisation of the actual city square, as opposed to the ritual open space incorporated into a single building entity, the result of comprehensive redevelopment, in faint-hearted imitation of the traditional square.

There are two aspects of this development that provoke some astonishment: the evenhandedness that allows the state to intervene without dictating every detail, leaving the development open to market opportunities without renouncing a central interest in preserving community values; and the fact that there appears to be a complete absence of ideological fervour the sort of either-or sectarianism that in London has produced a stiff confrontation between over-modern High-Tech and over-reactionary Classical Revival.

There is one aspect of all this that is especially unusual to the eyes of the architectural critic: the variety of the architectural interventions, some of which blend into the street architecture by their judicious use of brickwork, others of which stand out by their international whiteness and uncompromising newness. Cities are sites for the mutual definition of order and variety. At the level of the architects' persuasion and personal preferences, how has this marvellous combination of order and variety come about?

Perhaps it was in the coherence of a group of like-minded people that had the wit to club together to present a joint programme for a big project. If this is the case, we are still better off than if the competition had been won by a single large office, in which case the variety would have been largely simulated, or produced by design management: but these buildings are genuinely varied, in style as well as in formation. One is reminded of the strange case of the Festival of Britain, when Hugh Casson masterminded a conglomerate of different architects and had them cooperate to create the South Bank Exhibition, full of picturesque juxtaposition in the manner of the artist Gordon Cullen. At the time, young architects like myself, who were scornful of the very idea of managing variety, characterised the result as kitsch. Years later, Reyner Banham was able to show that a remarkable unity underlay that variety, perhaps simply the unity of the moment that was 1951. There seems to be a unity underlying the variety of the Temple Bar interventions. Perhaps it lies in a particular moment, the moment of the advent of the European horizon (inseparable from the moment of incurring excessive success in the Eurovision Song Contest). Perhaps it is a moment when modern architecture is finally absorbing the lessons of postmodernism, the realisation that all solutions are conditional, not absolute, that art—including architecture as art—is borne on the back of an invisible elephant, itself carried along on the back of an invisible tortoise, swimming in a sunless sea (an Indian myth on the nature of the cosmos, approximating to the Barthian idea of Culture as Container). Or it may be less momentous, a transitory pulse in the tide of fashion.

Certainly, there is a preponderance in these buildings of modern functional planning, the residue of a Corbusian aesthetic that combines a largely orthogonal room layout with the judicious use of curves at points of emphasis: some really neat planning. There are large windows, but the areas of plate glass stop short of being window walls. The principle elevations show combinations of openings of different sizes, rather than being made up of uniform repetitions. Buildings are sometimes broken into different parts and differentiated by the use of different materials. Internally, there is a flow of modern space, around corners and up through different floors, but a judicious use of separation and of separate rooms when appropriate. There is a lot of reinforced concrete civilised by the application of stucco. And almost all the window frames, staircases and elevator cages are in welded steel, which imparts a certain tough-mindedness along with the conversational flow.

Difficult for the critic to differentiate between so much excellence. I am particularly impressed by the resourcefulness of Shay Cleary Architects (the Multi-Media Centre) in the Curved Street, by an agile lightness of touch in the work of Derek Tynan (the Printworks—a mixed-use and residential building at East Essex Street), by the sense of archetype always dramatically present in the work of O'Donnell and Tuomey (the Irish Film Centre, the Photographic Archive). These are personal preferences, but every building I saw on a recent tour had something original and suggestive to offer.

It is quite remarkable that this feast of modern, useful and stylish buildings should come hand in hand with such care and even love for the pre-existing architecture of the city. Shay Cleary's Multi-Media Centre incorporates an old house, preserving enough to speak for it, without inhibiting the new spaces with which it communicates: an exercise in sheer tact. Shane O'Toole's Children's Centre in Eustace Street retains the complete street frontage of the old Quaker Meeting House, and insinuates behind it an extraordinary universe of Jack-and-the-beanstalk marvels, scaled to the world of the child. One of these marvels is the way the auditorium is transformed into a summer proscenium, the backcloth screen rises up to form an outward projecting canopy, and the building reveals to Meeting House Square its alter ego: modern architecture with a human face.

None of these buildings-in-the-city has compromised itself by a sentimental front or a dilution of its own convictions. Grafton Architects' north side to Temple Bar Square does not impose a classical ideal, but follows out an inner compulsion to explore asymmetry and abstracted balance: it nonetheless responds to its duty to provide the frontage that establishes a new square in the public realm. The mixture of public duty and private indulgence is somehow a mark of candour, a gauge of genuine feeling in a situation where many interests are at stake.

One is completely bemused by the sensitive way Austin Dunphy has preserved and restored an old 1733 house in Eustace Street, not ideologically committed to a doctrinaire and mythical ideal, but allowing the character of successive periods to appear as one progresses upward through the floors: a compromise that does not cheat history. Or one is agreeably diverted by Sean O'Laoire's Green Building, an experiment in environmental reconciliation that is also a stylish essay in street architecture on both its east and west faces.

Perhaps the clue to the overall success of these young architects lies in an earlier essay by Group '91, the polemical proposal contained in the exhibition titled "Making a Modern Street", which established at a theoretical level the principles that underlie the concrete results obtained in Temple Bar. Models of eight houses put side by side unequivocally form the image of a street. Each house speaks with an individual voice, yet the street that they aggregate is clearly a street. Modern voices add up to a traditional form. The result echoes, in a curious way, the Rue Mallet-Stevens in Paris, where a group of diverse avant-garde architects in the 20s succeeded in having some modern villas constructed, not in the ideal Modernist park, but in a street, the destination of 99 per cent of all taxi rides, the street that participates in the aggregate system of streets that we call the city.

Across the river from Temple Bar a large development has just been completed, under an entirely different system. The old Dublin is recaptured, not in spirit, but in appearance. Along Bachelors Walk the scale and plot divisions of the old quay have been restored by design management so that, from across the river, the past seems to have been retrieved. On closer inspection, this is the result of imitation, of the space of appearance. The result was foreseen, fore-ordained. In Temple Bar, a different method has led to more interesting and more genuine results. The life of the city has been extended, by renewing the system that gave rise to it in the first place. If it's not the last word, it's an ongoing show that commands our respect.

Is the result Irish? Not in any obvious way, but all the same it has a native quality: in the small scale and the unpretentiousness, in its improvisatory nature, in a certain quick-wittedness and conversational aplomb. It is certainly agreeable in the way that Dublin has always seemed agreeable: not overwhelming, not monothematic, but open-ended, personable, and incidentally providing the material for a literary narrative. As in Joyce's *Ulysses*. It provides a salutary lesson to government and people alike.

London, May 1996, published in Temple Bar, The Power of an Idea, edited Patricia Quinn, Gandom Editions 1996.

Margaret Dent's ashes, already sprinkled on rosebuds, are scattered from a fishing boat on the Solent; because of rough seas Andrew Preece makes a very short speech, and we return to port safely, 10 June.

A review of Robert Venturi's new book is published in the *Architectural Research Quarterly*, Cambridge.

ICONOGRAPHY AND ELECTRONICS UPON A GENERIC ARCHITECTURE
REVIEW FOR *ARQ*
Robert Venturi: *Iconography and Electronics upon a Generic Architecture: A View from the Drafting Room*, MIT Press, 1996

This book is a collection of Venturi's essays, lectures, letters, speeches, aphorisms and memorabilia. Several essays were written jointly with his partner, Denise Scott Brown, but the tone in every case is personal, revealing their private responses as well as standing up for themselves in public. They were mostly written since 1990, although there are a few from the 80s, and he has reprinted the text of "Learning from Aalto", an important essay from 1976, and has even resurrected his Master of Fine Arts Thesis at Princeton University of 1950. The intention of going back to his design thesis is evidently to show that it anticipates his subsequent career, and it clearly does. The essays amount to a vindication of the design approach that he launched with his first building—the headquarters for the North Penn Visiting Nurse Association—in 1961, and the theory that he launched with *Complexity and Contradiction in Architecture* in 1966. At the very least one has to acknowledge that theory and practice are all of a piece, and that Robert Venturi has been nothing if not consistent throughout a practice extending over a period of 35 years.

There is no new theory here, there has been no need to justify changes of course or transformations of style. What is new, perhaps, is that the polemic is no longer undertaken in order to refute Brutalism (the pseudo-sculptural style of Paul Rudolph in Crawford Mansions, which was the butt of his objections in *Learning from Las Vegas*, 1977), but to refute all unthinking modernism, including and particularly the pseudo-sculptural style of the deconstructivists. At the root of his position is a conviction that architecture as art is limited by its social duties, by its role of providing shelter for human occasions of all kinds, and by its practical responsibilities, the need to protect against the weather and the entropy of material degeneration. These considerations preclude its being an entirely free mode of expression: it has to pay attention to proprieties and limit its shock, when new.

Since the avant-garde position, whether in art or criticism, has always tended towards shock therapy, maximising the shock of the new in order to rock established positions, this brings Venturi up against the critics. They have not been kind to him; particularly British critics, who have castigated him as reactionary and effete, and for not being able to look in the face the future which they so ardently desire. One of the most telling pieces in the book is "J'adore St Paul's—a refutation of a British critic's piece J'accuse St Paul's", (*AD Profiles*, September–October 1993). The absurdity in that piece of criticising St Paul's for not being High-Tech might have led one to dismiss it as ideological drivel, but Venturi, like a caring teacher, takes us through the points one by one as if they could be taken seriously. This worry seems to stem from a certain paranoia, a feeling that critics get away with too much, and, moreover, don't have to agonise over design. (The volume is subtitled *A View from the Drafting Room.*) Venturi, who writes more than most architects, and to more effect, regards himself primarily as a working architect, one who happens to have studied his subject, including its history.

If we don't learn much more about the theory, we do learn a lot more about the architect Venturi, at grips with critics and journalists. He voices here his complaint against the architecture critic at the *Philadelphia Inquirer*, for substituting an unflattering snapshot of the Clinical Research building on the Penn campus for the professionally skilled view supplied: this letter was never sent, so there is an aspect here of settling old scores before it is too late. He complains to Herbert Muschamp about his comments in the *New York Times* on the Whitehall Ferry Terminal, while asking him not to publish the letter. A marvellous letter to William and Mary Ellen Bowen (the ex-President of Princeton University and his wife), who are proposing to visit the Sainsbury Wing in London, warns them about all the things that went wrong, mostly due to British pigheadedness, including the omission of a hose bib in the entrance porch to save £100. There are protests sent to competition committees and pieces published in justification of their designs for the Philadelphia Concert Hall, which came under attack for being provincial, for not being in the league of *Les Grands Projets* of Paris in addressing its site on the newly named Avenue of the Arts (formerly Broad Street). In this piece Venturi draws on the American inheritance of homespun self-reliance as a way of justifying his own kind of building, which, as already with Guild House in 1964, prefers relatively cheap applied ornament to expensive sculptural form. It is impossible not to sympathise with an architect who is condemned by his own polemic to fight simultaneously on two fronts.

For while he rejects sculptural DECON in favour of the straightforward decorated shed, (now known as the decorated generic building) he also rejects retro-modernism that tries to extend the life of the white-walled buildings of the 30s (presumably therefore work like that of Richard Meier). As he rightly points out, the modern style based on an industrial warehouse aesthetic evolved about one hundred years ago, so that the act of continuing it today is as much backward looking as it is a continued anticipation of a mythical future. In any case the future that utopian Modernism expected in the 30s has not come about: is that not something from which we should learn? In chiding the retro-modernists, Venturi tends to treat them as stupid or scurrilous rather than mistaken, and in this he seems to lack understanding for the way ordinary people continue to fall for future-hype. The state-of-the art product is something that the ordinary person wants, whether in cars, cameras, hi-fi or CD-ROMs, and the current popularity of the mobile phone testifies to this hunger for the new. To this kind of ordinary person the qualities of modesty and common sense that he claims for his own buildings are all but invisible. That his facades are laced with electronic glitter is hardly registered, because electric signs are part of normal life, and where they are situated is a matter of indifference. Venturi's boldness in applying them to serious buildings is, I suspect, a form of protest, not a popularist venture.

Theory in architecture is a strange animal, it has very little to do with theory in science, which aims to be predictive. Theory in art has become more and more a form of proselytising for a carefully positioned avant-garde stance addressed to fellow avant-gardists. On the model of Vitruvius, theory in architecture was a mixture of mastery of the past and practical hints for the future. Perhaps Le Corbusier's book *Vers une architecture* changed all that; with its plea for a vision of the future it was above all a polemic. One cannot say that Le Corbusier predicted the future so much as helped to bring it about. Venturi's theory has had an equal, if gentler, polemical success. "As I travel I see elements of buildings from my hotel window that originated in my/our work and have been exploited all over the world", reads the title of one of his complaints. He is not thrilled to be the source of imitation, and must be constantly on guard to fight off the claims of his imitators, as if they had stolen useful commissions.

It is clear from the examples he chose in *Complexity and Contradiction* that Robert Venturi enjoys complexity and contradiction, and hence the game of self-contradiction that defines Mannerist architecture. I share that enjoyment, as I find it in Romano and Hawksmoor, but I confess that I don't find it so much in the work of Venturi. To enjoy transgression, it is first necessary to believe in sin. The thing to be contradicted has to be strong, so that it lends its weight to the subversion of it. A sensible, practical architecture for our age does not in itself provide that weight; indeed the conditions of contemporary American practice, where the desired marketable image is hung out on a quickly erected steel frame, make all forms of surface play equally sensible and equally short-lived.

This suggests that his theory is less important in his own practice, and in the practice of others, than unspoken and unverified matters of taste. His theory is sufficiently general to support many different sensibilities in the interpretation of it. While one may admire Venturi and Denise for their boldness then, one finds it difficult to sympathise with their outrage now. Only they can produce an authentic Venturi building, and an abundance of cheap imitations should in principle reflect their glory. Did Corb complain about cheap imitations? Their theory was effective, perhaps because it anticipated a real cultural shift, the eventual demise of the functionalist myth.

London, 30 May 1996, published ARQ, summer 1996, and Times Higher Educational Supplement, 18 July 1997.

B contributes to *The Dictionary of Art*, London and New York: Macmillan. RM External Examiner at Cambridge, dinners at King's College, Robinson College, 20 to 21 June.

Reception and flat warming by the Portes in their new penthouse, where Celia was architect, 28 June.

Memorial service for Dorothy Rowe at Oxford, and lunch with David: we feel he's been fair, 22 June.

Colin Rowe: *As I was Saying: miscellaneous memoirs and essays* (3 vols).

RM introduces van Heyningen and Haward for their presentation at the RIBA, 2 July.

INTRODUCTION OF VAN HEYNINGEN AND HAWARD
RIBA

It's a pleasure to have been asked to introduce our speakers tonight: I've known both of them for quite some time.

In 1959, when I was Second Year Master at the AA, Birkin was in my class, along with some others due to distinguish themselves professionally, including Chris Woodward, Edward Jones, Michael Hopkins. There was in force an unspoken agreement that drawings should be precise, that lines should indicate unambiguously the edge of every plane, outline the essential volumes and be in black ink on white paper. Some wonderful drawings were made, and that was well before computers.

Joanna I met a little later, early 70s I think, when I was invited as visiting critic to Cambridge, to review one of Birkin's studios there. I remember this design that caught my eye, with its stylishly rounded corners. I was introduced to Joanna, whose own stylishly rounded corners also made a deep impression. So I can say that if Joanna was once Birkin's student, Birkin was once my student.

Birkin taught as well at the Royal College of Art and at the Bartlett. But he also worked a long apprenticeship, first with Harlow New Town, then for 14 years with Norman Foster, where he worked on the Sainsbury Centre, Willis Faber, the Hammersmith Project. I saw quite a lot of Birkin during the late 70s, when my wife Celia Scott was also working on Hammersmith. I used to go into the office in Charlotte Street and say "Hello", rather loudly, and a forest of heads would instantly appear above the five foot high work station screens, making it easy to work out one's route.

Joanna served a much shorter apprenticeship, with Neylan and Ungless. After three years of being told what to do, and a short interval spent with Michael Hopkins, she left to set up her own practice. That was in 1977, the year she and Birkin got married. One forms the distinct impression that Joanna does not relish being told what to do, nor even having Birkin being told what to do. In 1983 she persuaded Birkin to throw in his lot with her, and thus they formed van Heyningen and Haward.

I won't detail the work of their practice: in a moment, they will speak for it, and it will speak for itself. Their work is always marked by clarity of conception and precision of detail. It is fundamentally modern in these respects, conveying economy and lightness. I would say that it is classically modern. The geometry is studied as obsessively as the dimensional system. The debt to Foster is there, but when I think of the Sainsbury Centre—my favourite Foster building—I also see Foster's debt to Haward. Anyway, the idea of a strict, reticent shed with grand porches at either end is about to resurface with the design of their new offices in a genuinely old shed.

As people, they make a strong claim on one's friendship. Birkin has the apparent vagueness of someone who is always following out an internal argument. Joanna has the brightness of someone who wants to know what's going on, even if its not the best news. Birkin is cautious. Joanna is forthright. Birkin has an eye for beauty, Joanna has a gift for friendship. Together, they complement one another, they have the stability of a team that allows ideas to be worked out every which way. They meditate their work thoroughly.

And I think that you will see that this ability to meditate on the outcome is having an effect on their work, which is all the time getting more serious and more thoughtful. One remembers that James Stirling was greatly impressed with their Rare Books Library at Newnham, which, he said, had presence. It's to do with creating a modern architecture that is not temporary and in transition, but that contributes something permanent of value to the environment; an aim that I also used to attribute to Stirling. In these terms, their work commands our respect as well as our admiration.

Ladies and Gentlemen, I give you Birkin and Jo!

London, July 1996.

Michael Wilford speaks at RIBA, we have drinks before at Valerie, and afterwards supper with Mary Stirling at Pizza House, 9 July.

RM gives lunch at the Athenaeum to Luca Molinari, client for the Skira book (Writings of JS), 10 July.

Holiday in France: Paris Hotel de L'Academie, then a trip to Puyloubier, 18 July to 7 August.

We go to La Gaffe for dinner with Wayland and Jeannot, the Jacottets, Eleanor and Jeanie, 27 July.

To Aix for supermarket. Campari-sodas at Les Deux Garçons, then home for rabbit cooked by C, 29 July.

We go to Claviers to hear Léon Krier and his new wife perform in the church: Léon's piano splendid, 5 August.

We take Mary out for dinner at *Le Bien Etre*. We visit Le Thoronet on way to Marseille, 7 August.

Visit Stephen Spender's studio at Malden, Sussex, a modern use of steel, 1 September.

Lunch at Athenaeum to Ricky Burdett and Antoine Grumbach, who was over for the *Bridges* Competition, 4 September.

Trip to Bristol to meet Sasha Lubetkin, tea on way back with Mandy and Barney, 11 September.

SOUNDS AND SWEET AIRS AT STUTTGART
REVIEW FOR *RIBA JOURNAL*

The Stirling-Wilford Urban Plan for the area adjoining their celebrated Staatsgalerie extension has moved another big step towards completion with the opening of the Music School. This leaves unbuilt only the L-shaped block near the middle of the original development plan, intended to complete an urban square to provide a site for the celebrated Fountain of Destiny, facing the State Opera house on the opposite side of Konrad Adenauer Street. The development plan envisaged this street, which at the moment is virtually an urban freeway, being put into a tunnel, allowing a landscaped strip above it to provide uninhibited pedestrian access to the park and onward to the pedestrianised city centre. This would complete in explicit form the pedestrian network coming from high up the northern slope of the city, and passing through the circular court of the Staatsgalerie, or alternatively through the garden at the foot of the new tower of the Music School.

The unfinished section was originally to have been an independent Theatre Academy. The needs of the Staatsgalerie, and now of the new Music School, for additional accommodation, are such as to preclude the completion of this phase in its original form, but the building as determined by the shape of the civic square could just as easily absorb ancillary accommodation. The architects have demonstrated its flexibility in several proposals. The Land Government has indicated its support for what ultimately will be an infill project, but action will clearly have to await the end of the period of financial stringency imposed by the Maastricht deadline for monetary unity.

These uncertainties are perhaps inseparable from an extensive project of this size. It is not a matter of a single building, but of a coherent shaping of the city. The urban design aspect of the project is as important as its architectural quality, for it demonstrates the successful integration of building and environment according to James Stirling's stated criteria, which have been recently reiterated by Michael Wilford in his lecture at the RIBA. To demonstrate a Modernism which does not fetishise the isolated building seems to be an important achievement of the Stirling-Wilford approach to architecture.

The most evident feature of this stage of the completed design is the substantial cylindrical tower in the middle of the building, designed by the architects to take its place as one of the many "stubby towers" that are characteristic of the city. From the roof terrace of the tower there is a splendid view of the park and the city centre, and the tower itself is visible across the park, at least from the margin of the pedestrianised centre, so there is a strong sense of connection and fulfilment at the urban design scale.

Architecturally, the tower is as imposing as the drawings promised. It can be said that the close collaboration between the partners and the total integration of their design team have allowed another key building to be brought to completion with all its power intact. To Stirling it represented the "cork" ejected from the champagne celebration of the Staatsgalerie courtyard, and it is sad to think that he has been denied the satisfaction of seeing this conceit realised. Not only does it make a relation formally to the central drum of the Staatsgalerie, it continues the somewhat meditative theme set up there. The tower terminates in a remarkable coved cornice that echoes the cornice on the Staatsgalerie. In response to the vegetation already engulfing the court of the Staatsgalerie in an atmosphere of Piranesian doom, it raises against the sky windowless openings that suggest a gutted interior, and that can just as easily be seen to speak of poetic retribution. Yet the way in which these openings invade the curve of the cornice projects an image that is far from Neoclassical in its import, and indeed is totally unexpected and highly original.

The tower is also effective as an element of the interior. Projecting as it does from the south wall of the building, it partly blocks the view of the adjoining open space, while yet allowing that space to breathe, because its attachment is narrower than its bulk. It effectively liberates the building into the sunlight, while providing all the action on the side that lies towards the city. The cylinder of the tower subsumes a variety of room arrangements within it and the way in which the circular space has been allocated to different uses at different levels demonstrates a wonderful versatility. The lecture room at the lowest level, the main auditorium above it, then the library on two levels immediately above that, the two floors of practice rooms, and finally the roof terrace are all connected into the rectangular layout of the main building in ways that demonstrate great tactical aplomb. As a result, the form of the tower, clearly chosen because of its potential in the cityscape, is not felt as an incubus within the building as a whole. Because our perception of size is affected by proportion, the tower dissimulates the existence of the auditorium, and as a result this seems unexpectedly grand when one penetrates into it.

It is a splendid auditorium, immediately calling to mind the auditorium in the Cornell Center for the Performing Arts in its intimacy. Stirling thought of that hall as ideal for small-scale opera (he hoped it would be perfect for Mozart). This hall is excellent for music, its resonance balanced by its relatively small capacity, so that it plays warm. At the opening ceremony it demonstrated its suitability for both classical (Beethoven, Mendelssohn) and for modern (in this case a sigh-and-sneeze piece for 13 singers and percussion). The acoustic warmth is reinforced by the use of strong earth colours and concealed lighting, and the focus on the players is emphasised by the organ placed on axis, and reinforced by a ring of large columns on the back wall which act as a sort of metaphoric audience. The outsize light shades double as Egyptian capitals, cousins of the mushroom columns at the Performing Arts Center, and link us back to the poetic character of the tower as townscape: it adds up to a hall of character that reiterates the power of the building, and emphasises not physical attributes alone, but a more general quality, perhaps the spiritual quest that might ideally animate the aspirations of the young musician.

London, 20 June 1996, published September 1996.

London, Anniversary dinner at Le Caprice. Then go to the Architectural Foundation for Ricky Burdett's goodbye, 27 September.

B finishes work on front garden—wood edging and gravel infill, 4 October.

Lecture: *The New Expressionism*, for The RA Seminar on Art & Architecture.

RM to *Dictionary of Art* launch at the Banqueting House in Whitehall, 23 October.

RM lectures for the Twentieth Century Society at the AA: *the Schröder House Puzzle*, 26 October.

B introduces Jim Cadbury-Brown for his lecture at the AA, 20 November.

RM to Piran, Slovenia, for Piran's Days of Architecture Lecture: *Sixties Architecture in Britain* in Piran, Slovenia, 29 November to 1 December.

Lecture: *Functionalism and the Avant-Garde*, given at Tech Universität Berlin, Tech Universität Cottbus.

B joins in a personal tour of the Jewish Museum, led by Danny's wife Nina. He takes his own pics, December.

Charles Jencks hosts a lunch at the Athenaeum for Norman Foster, P Davey. Peter Palumbo fails to come, 18 December.

RM and C visit a built work of David Chipperfield, *The Rowing Museum* at Henley, December.

ROWING MUSEUM AT HENLEY
BY DAVID CHIPPERFIELD ARCHITECTS
REVIEW FOR *DOMUS*

In the gloom of a winter day, the long sheds of the Rowing Museum blend with the flat river landscape, bringing a touch of industrial scale, something like a small boat dockyard or a suburban railway station, to river edges that are otherwise cluttered with tacky and sentimental incidents. The plain wooden surfaces have the bulk of traditional barns, but are far too precise to be mistaken for vernacular buildings. Their solidity is poised with demanding exactitude above glass walls giving on to wooden terraces lined by plain glass balustrades. We are clearly confronted by the transparency that we have come to associate with exemplary modern buildings, we are in a highly charged situation where the conditions of our visit are challenged in advance by an environment which has been subjected to the demands of total design; we are skirting a danger zone where the terms of life have been redefined; in short, we are visiting a museum.

The barn-like forms no doubt served the architect as a means of accommodation to the pressures of local susceptibilities, in an area considered hallowed by tradition and the wearing of old school ties. They provided the Trojan horse within which the weapons of visual acuity were already being sharpened for the onslaught. And it appears that this strategy has been successful, for when the client subsequently decided to extend the accommodation by adding a second building, it was no longer necessary to camouflage it as another barn, it could stand out as a totally abstracted box, bereft of roof, tied into the first by the use of the same materials, and by the same demanding visual aesthetic.

To some who see the method of modernity as a crusade, which must always challenge normal expectations, the use here of vernacular profiles already savours of compromise, compounds a sort of betrayal. To these eyes, it seems pointless to use roof forms that employ steel structure and are covered with terne-coated stainless steel, but that look as if they have been there forever. In England today, the polemic between traditionalist and modernist is still defined in black and white, as mutually exclusive ways of life, as moral opposites; and there have been murmurs of disapprobation for a design that blends these opposites, however effectively.

However, the forms that on the outside appear as barn-like silhouettes are also the means of providing internal spaces ideally suited to the display of boats and boating. Luminosity drifts down from high rooflights, partly screened by baffles, and bathes the flat floor in a dim religious light, where the rowing shells will take on the mystery of objects in which history and technology come to terms. These are beautiful spaces, and if we turn to ask how rooflights could be raised to exactly this height to achieve exactly this luminous effect, the barn-like silhouette takes on a certain inevitability. On a city site, with high construction on all sides, the relationship could have been dovetailed into a complex building: here it simply has to be constructed in the open, raised up visibly, and with economy. But the result is imbued with a resonance, not only the shadow of a Medieval barn, but the shadow of a Medieval barn reconsidered by Louis Kahn, as at the Kimbell Museum. So the result is not only a physical presence, but a moral one, one that is fully aware of the project of modernity and of the problems of achieving it within cultural complexity.

Modernist buildings, as conceived in the heroic era, were bent on avoiding the arbitrary and retrieving truth. They were attempts to discover a fundamental relationship between form and content, the result of a transcendental purpose that could not be denied, just as certain organic objects like spiders' webs and snail shells could be considered beautiful in human terms simply because they followed bare necessity. In them, nothing was false, because nothing was added. The human designer could hope to emulate this transparency only by following bare necessity, and in the era of functionalism this became the doctrine of form following function. The true and frank expression of a functional need would automatically create its own sort of beauty. This expectation still to a degree attends the sort of architectural design that closely follows engineering principles, and it is this expectation that clouds the understanding of style, and that makes of the High-Tech style a fetish as much as a method.

For many architects, it is difficult even today to relinquish this expectation, when everything else combines to persuade us that our willingness to accept necessity is equalled only by our insistence on moulding it to our wishes. Between the bare necessity and our enjoyment of it there intervenes the whole cultural realm of expression, and this is invariably influenced by our beliefs and aspirations, by our ideological goals. It is only when warmed by an ideological purpose that we can believe in the transparency of our motives.

David Chipperfield has distinguished himself early in his career by the way he has given serious consideration to the very conditions of style in architecture. This is not to say that he is simply a stylist, but that he has pondered the problematic nature of expression, and come to terms intelligently with the ambiguous nature of poetic truth. In his architecture, we are given elementary forms that, in the first place, suggest their uses, and then, in a magical way, bring those uses into the realm of ritual. His buildings are undoubtedly modernist, accepting the abstract forms that were invented in Europe during the 20s, making of them a vocabulary out of which a whole life-style may be constructed. They are also minimalist, and it is possible to see now that the development of modern art throughout the course of the twentieth century has changed the perception of what minimalist forms mean and of what minimalist architecture can attempt to encompass. Then, it was about a limitation of technique that would produce economy of construction, and the adoption of standardisation that would make available a universal method. Now, it is about renewing the act of living by cleansing the perception. Chipperfield thus addresses himself to the unfinished Modernist project, with a subtlety that is only equalled by his directness.

London, 20 December 1996.

1997

A musical evening with Max Steuer. Goodbye to Effie. Great jazz, 23 January.

B introduces Patrick Hodgkinson for Twentieth Century Society Lecture, Cowcross St, 27 February.

RM gives a lecture at the Royal Academy on *Architecture as Expression*, March 1997.

TRANSGRESSIONS:
CROSSING THE LINES AT THE ROYAL ACADEMY
ARCHITECTURE AS EXPRESSION:
CAN IT APPROACH THE CONDITION OF ART?

The Modern Movement in architecture was a continuation of rationalist aspirations that first took shape in the eighteenth century, and the hard-edged white prisms of Le Corbusier and Terragni have roots in the pure geometrical forms of Boullée and Ledoux. The difference is that, largely through the impact of abstraction, architectural forms have been liberated from the duty to represent propriety through convention, and hence from the domination of the classical orders. But they still are temperamentally on the side of strong light and high definition, what we might call the light side of art, and consistent with the idea that art produces a radiance.

But the light side is only apparent because there is a dark side. There is another tradition, that also has its roots in the eighteenth century, but which develops in a different direction, by way of probing the limits of lightness, and the edge of the dark. It may seem paradoxical that the eighteenth century, the Age of Enlightenment, should produce Piranesi, who was fascinated by the disappearance of the past, by ruins and by prisons. But he is as much part of the Enlightenment as was the Marquis de Sade. In both we see a search for the limits of the darkness. In the succeeding Romantic movement, this search gains in confidence and in power of expression, and gives a new value to darkness, as for example in qualities attributed by Baudelaire to cats: "*Amis de la science, et de la volupté/ ils cherchent le silence et l'horreur des ténèbres*".

This tradition took shape through the worship of the sublime, that limit where human values become insignificant, and there is a continuous line that develops through the Romantics and the French *Décadents* to the German Expressionists. It's not unfair to call this the dark side of art: not just because it favours intuition in place of the reasoned position, but because it positively cultivates the irrational. If the system that holds us in life is weak, we need to know where it will break down. And the artist likes to remind us of human mortality, of the closure which awaits us all, and the need therefore to avoid a too easy closure in art. Hence our love of the macabre, of simulated terror, of romantic excess, where Eros desires an impossible outcome analogous to the Christian concept of eternal life.

There is a sense in which this side of human nature has been reinforced by the development of science, with its trust in rational procedures, because it seems to attach

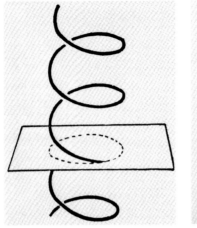

Spiral
Hinton, 1904

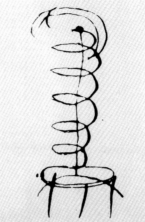

Spiral
Marcel Duchamp, 1934

to all those things that remain mysterious in spite of the discoveries of science, that is, to the unknown. The unknown is the dark edge of the known. But the rational only covers a very small domain, and most of life remains outside of it. This is evident in Duchamp's response to Hinton's *Spiral Intersecting a Plane*, which he calls *Handler of Gravity*. In the early years of this century, scientific ideas based on N-dimensional geometry produced among artists a fever about the Fourth Dimension, analogous to our fever about virtual reality. Charles Howard Hinton's book *The Fourth Dimension*, of 1904, was a principal cause of this. The unknown has always exerted a deep fascination for us, and is, in a sense, the source of all art, since art is as much concerned with disturbing order that is too complete as with making a fresh, an as yet unknown, order. Good art of course does both.

Around the year 1907, with the development of Cubism, abstraction began to produce forms that were no longer imitated from nature, but reflected the artist's feelings in front of nature. It was Paul Cézanne who prepared the way for this transformation. Cézanne still interrogates his motif, the evidence of his eyes, but he has taken certain freedoms to produce an equivalent, not a copy. The Cubists went further in this direction. After Cubism and De Stijl the artist's gesture was completely liberated. Art became gestural, and with this new flexibility shapes on the canvas could become the direct expression of the artist's feelings.

By the 50s, when art began to centre on New York, instead of Paris, the liberation of the gesture reached another stage. Now we see the actual marks of the paint, the gesture itself makes the final form, the form arises through the actual movement of the artist's arm; we have reached the era of Abstract Expressionism. In fine art then, the artist was entirely liberated to express feeling. But in architecture, by what now seems a questionable development, a similar freedom from convention led to a new tyranny—the tyranny of function. The new, the unexpected, which the artist could seek inside his own subjectivity, for the architect had to come from outside. His subjectivity was dangerous ground for someone who claimed to be following function. It was safer to attribute new ideas to the science side, and so to justify them from a world of facts.

Drawing for a Glass House
Hans Scharoun, 1920

Cubic Exhibition Building
Wenzel Hablik, 1921

Moreover, what the artist may do gesturally on a sheet of paper, has to go through a social and technical process if it is to emerge as a built work. The emphasis on expression, as opposed to a rational emphasis on the building process, has the effect of privileging the gesture over the construction. The building task as a rational process requiring communication across a team, may bring a certain loss of expression. It is interesting to compare Wenzel Hablik's Cubic Exhibition Building of 1921 with Hans Scharoun's Drawing for a Glass House, of the previous year. In both cases we have a glass tower, diminishing upwards, and crowned by diagonals. Scharoun's free gesture in pen and ink has to be transposed into a set of forms suitable for building in stages. It regains its freedom by dislocation of the expected geometry.

It is a question of great interest how the impact of abstraction, which had such a strong effect in twentieth century painting, was not matched within architecture. Between the free gesture and the constructed reality lay a space: the space of functionality. Buildings had to be responsive to the uses and activities they were to shelter, and they had to be constructed more or less economically according to the technological resources of the times. So they tended to come out as rectangular boxes. To get round these constraints, and still present the result as artistic, required an idealisation of the programme and the act of construction, and this is what gave rise to what I have called the *Myths of Space and Function* in the theory of Modernist architecture. Both of these aspects were distorted far from reality.

Alpine Architecture
Bruno Taut, 1919

Project: *Club for the Peak, Hong Kong*
Zaha Hadid,1982

However, there was a brief moment in the early 20s, when architects of the Russian Revolution could claim to be both avant-garde artists and constructors of the new reality. The abstraction that had liberated the artist, at last began to liberate the architect.

Today, we see a remarkable change, in which at last an attempt seems to be made to free architectural forms from rectangular constraints and return to the early 20s in spirit. Zaha Hadid's drawing of 1982 for her project for a club on the Peak at Hong Kong, seems to hark back to Bruno Taut's fantasy called Alpine Architecture, of 1919. In both cases, in order to make the link between natural and artificial forms, the mountains and the buildings are merged together in the drawing. Nature is idealised in the same direction as the architecture. In her drawings for Planetary Architecture, of 1987, Hadid seemed to be referring to Malevich's drawings for Suprematist Architecture. The drawings, although deriving from

Project: *Palace of the Soviets*
Konstantin Melnikov, 1932

Jewish Museum, Berlin (site model)
Daniel Libeskind, 1993–1995

the rectangular volumes of the Modern Movement, express an architecture that is so free that it escapes from gravity. It is clearly in the realm of art—abstract, weightless. Her boldness lies precisely in the fact that she does not compromise with conventions, but behaves as an artist, following her gesture. The fire station at Weil am Rhein showed that she could get the gesture built, although not without somewhat changing its effect.

Le Corbusier relates how he refused a commission to design a church, sometime in the 20s, because he didn't see how the sort of abstract forms he was exploring could be used in a symbolic role. By 1951, when he designed Ronchamp, he had revised this view. But the Russians never had any problem with symbolism. In his design of 1932 for a Palace of the Soviets, Melnikov goes straight from the abstract to the symbolic. The building expands upwards, it consists of a pyramid accompanied by an inverted pyramid. The meaning intended to cancel out the conventional pyramid with the ruler on top and the mass of people suppressed at the base; now, the people were to be on top, and we are witnessing a liberation. Built form does not readily lend itself to this kind of symbolisation: the building looks more like a sort of rocket launcher.

More successful is a piece of modern symbolism that works through the juxtaposition of spaces, as in Daniel Libeskind's Jewish Museum in Berlin. The main gallery is laid out in a zigzag, based on part of the Jewish six-pointed star, crossing and re-crossing a kind of mausoleum space below, into which one cannot enter, but only sense it as a forbidden world. This is potentially a very powerful way of expressing strong feeling. The memorial space is a high volume poorly lit by reflected light from a single opening at the top. To visit it is to be momentarily imprisoned. It is outside the heating system, so the cold you feel tells you something of the rejection that must have been felt by the victims of Nazism: this is design by empathy.

Villa Dall'Ava
Rem Koolhaas, 1990

Villa Dall'Ava—another view
Rem Koolhaas

Hadid began her career with OMA—the Office for Metropolitan Architecture—with Rem Koolhaas and Elia Zenghelis. Koolhaas is another who has used architectural drawing to liberate himself from convention. We can compare his Observation Tower in a Rotterdam Project with El Lissitzky's Speaker's Platform, of 1920. So he too takes a leaf from the Russian Constructivists, although in his case, he has not abandoned the desire to build.

In his subsequent work he has kept quite close to the prismatic forms made canonic by their association with the Modern Movement. But at the same time he has subjected these prismatic forms to a peculiar kind of subversion, so that instead of looking rational, they look arbitrary, the result of unconscious irony or subconscious machination. In this way, by frustrating our, by now, normal expectations of functionalist architecture, Koolhaas restores us to a world of feeling.

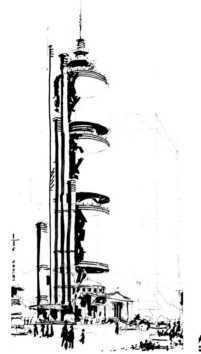

Project in Seattle
Richard Rogers, 1984

A Call for Industrialisation
Chernikhov, 1929

Richard Rogers is commonly seen as representative of a rational, functional architecture that uses high technology to solve physical problems. You could say that he romanticises industrial forms, including oil refineries. The Modern Movement began by romancing the steel, and Rogers kept to this ideology, to the point of proposing a necklace of industrial forms along the Thames, in his proposal *London as it could be*. But maybe on closer examination he yearns also for the mantle of the avant-garde artist. Compare his Project for Seattle of 1984 with Chernikhov's *A call for industrialisation* of 1929, and you will see some connection. Where Koolhaas goes back to the heroic period in a spirit of irony, Rogers goes back with his enthusiasm intact.

In Norman Foster's Hongkong and Shanghai Bank everything is apparently rational and technical, except that a good deal of accident is allowed to enter in, perhaps so as to

Apartment Complex, Vienna
Coop Himmelb(l)au, 1983

Hongkong and Shanghai Bank, interior
Norman Foster, 1986

stand in for the idea of freedom, or stimulus. The space in which the escalators rise into the atrium provides us with a rich variety of juxtapositions, producing an effect which is not so far removed from the accidental look that Coop Himmelb(l)au, the Viennese architects, deliberately cultivate as a form of expression. So the High-Tech school is slipping into the current revaluing of Expressionism.

In the modern architecture of the 20s, the attempt to bring science and technology to bear went along with rational procedures and standardisation. For instance, steel fabrication was not thought to be economic unless you achieved what were called "economies of scale", and that meant repetition of standard dimensions. Today, computer technology allows all the parts of a building to be individually different. Frank Gehry pioneered computerised control of fabrication with his design for the Guggenheim Museum in Bilbao. Similarly, Nick Grimshaw was able to have the parts of his Chunnel Terminal at Waterloo varied so that the overall form could conform to the sweep of the curves determined accidentally by the site plan. At the same time, by adopting a three-pinned arch structure, he could make the structure disappear halfway across, so that the space seems due to a structural miracle instead of structural rationality. So the rectangular boxes once thought to be part of rational control have given way to more sophisticated methods, and architecture is now free to follow the expressive gesture in a way it never was before.

In the middle of plenty we have poverty; in the middle of everyday life we have the horror of the terrorist bomb. Contrasts, and a danger that may come without warning, are what we now have to contend with. The 'New Expressionism' in architecture, to coin a phrase, is concerned not only with claiming the freedom of the artist, the space of the gesture. It seeks to question the limits of Enlightenment, the edge beyond which our power does not go, the closeness of strangeness, the loss of the familiar. Many architects feel the need to respond to the unfamiliar, making a kind of architecture that tries to express the opposite of what buildings normally do: the uncertainty of the postmodern condition.

So Lebbeus Woods wants to express impatience with the excessive rationality of the German state, and its tendency to impose a too rigid order, as many would see in the planning controls exercised by the city authorities in Berlin. His Berlin Free-Zone— freespace section makes a sharp contrast between order and disorder, and here the

Berlin Free-Zone: Free-space section
Lebbeus Woods, 1990

A bomb explodes
Northern Ireland

expression of disorder is equated with violence. What looks like disorder becomes freedom, what looks like order becomes servitude. His Zone of Freedom rips through the frame of a conventional building like a bomb going off. Compare this with an actual bomb going off in Northern Ireland.

Underground Berlin, Alexanderplatz
Lebbeus Woods, 1988

Lima, Peru: an improvised shanty

The image of dissolution which opposes itself to the excessive order of our presumably oppressive governments is matched by the unwanted dissolution of our cities. There is a world of difference between the forms employed by the artist to express dissolution and the experience of the dissolute life of a city slum, as here in Lima, Peru. To be subjected to this life where crime has become normal must be an ordeal; for the artist, to represent the forms of a dissolving order is a search for freedom. As always with fugitive meanings, we have to recognise that the state of freedom is subjective, and that the adoption of conventions so as to be able to communicate at all, while it involves a loss of subjective freedom, represents a gain in commonality and so in liberty. Architecture may approach the condition of art, but so long as it is inhabited, it has other duties as well.

London, 8 March 1997, published Architectural Design, July/August 1997.

Kurt Forster's lecture at the AA, coming home we encounter fire engines, find that no. 5 Mall Studios has been burnt down, and its tenant, Hans, is dead. Since he was nearly blind, and lived alone, with a butt-end constantly in his mouth, this is hardly surprising, but still shocking, 28 January.

We attend dinner by Sandy and MJ in their studio: meet Ron Kitaj, Richard Hamilton, 14 March.

Published: *The Two-way Stretch—Between Past and Future* in *The Journal of Architecture*, spring.

Lectures: *Functionalism and the Avant-Garde* at Syracuse University, *The New Expressionism* at Cornell.

Paris, Hotel Trianon: visit Parc Citroën, Japan Centre; to Françoise Choay for dinner, 14/16 April.

RM introduces John Tuomey for his lecture at the RIBA; dinner with party at the Union Cafe, 29 April.

INTRODUCTION FOR JOHN TUOMEY
RIBA

John Tuomey was born in Tralee in 1954 and graduated from University College Dublin in 1976. He then worked in London in the office of Stirling-Wilford, taking part in the designing for the Staatsgalerie in Stuttgart and the Science Centre in Berlin. In 1980 he returned to Dublin, and worked at the Office of Public Works. In 1988 he set up an independent practice in partnership with Sheila O'Donnell. At the outset they were somewhat influenced by Stirling's potent mixture of Le Corbusier and Neoclassicism, and traces of Aldo Rossi can also be found. But since their beginning, their practice has developed in a very interesting and creative way, turning back towards a canonic Modernism, while at the same time attempting to engage in a dynamic relationship with the form of the city.

John has exhibited his work in the Sense of Ireland exhibition and *ManSpace* in London and at the Independent Artists Exhibition and the Blue Studio Gallery in Dublin. He has been published in several English magazines and has taught at University College London and has been the life and soul of the External Examiners at the Architectural Association.

In 1991 Dublin benefitted from a new initiative, a joint venture by the City of Dublin and a private development agency called Temple Bar Properties. Temple Bar Properties has been partly funded by the state, but given the freedom to raise private funding as well, and to pursue its aims of cultural regeneration without undue interference. A competition was organised with the aim of exploring ways of restructuring the Temple Bar, then a somewhat run-down area lying between Trinity College and the river Liffey. The competition produced 12 interesting entries drawn from large and small architectural studios, and it is perhaps a happy augury that it was won by a group of young architects who had combined specifically to take part in the competition, under the name of Group '91. John Tuomey and Sheila O'Donnell were leading members of this group.

The result to date is a marvellous renaissance of urban design. We find here new buildings that are strictly modern in style, often white-walled, which nevertheless contribute in a lively and enjoyable way to the form and to the vitality of the city. The Irish Film Centre and the Photographic Archive are the particular contributions of O'Donnell and Tuomey, and I hope we shall see some of this tonight.

The recent development of Barcelona to match the challenge of the Olympics has set an example of a city that is being regenerated through the addition of thoroughly modern buildings. Dublin is setting another example, one that London should learn from.

London, 29 April 1997.

Italian trip for lecture at Salerno: we visit the Grotte di Pertosa, Ravello, finally get inside the Villa Malaparte, 28 April.

In spite of the flat roof, which is special, it is not so modern, it speaks more of tradition.

But is full of very individual ideas like the open fireplace where the back is of glass, and the steps to the roof.

Lecture: *The Future of London* for the Ordine degli Architetti of Salerno, Italy, April.

We are impressed by the continuance of the passeggiata, in both directions, seafront, one street back.

This leads to an easy response to a request from *Architecture Today* for *My Kind of Town*.

MY KIND OF TOWN: AIX-EN-PROVENCE
FOR *ARCHITECTURE TODAY*

France has always exerted a special pull, ever since a three-week spell in Boulogne-sur-Mer at the age of 15, when I fell in love momentarily with a Swedish girl in the same boarding house. She was a little older, and her knowledge of French was superior to mine, but she seemed to enjoy practising it on me. From then on, French language became permanently suffused with glamour, to the extent that Colin Rowe, speaking on the occasion of his receiving the Royal Gold Medal at the RIBA, was able to characterise me as irredeemably Frenchified. Family holidays in Normandy confirmed the French taste, not so much in the consumption of food and wine, as in the unending puzzle of the cultural assumptions encountered, so similar, yet so different. Later, trips in a more architectural mode to check out the bastides of Aquitaine initiated a fascination with the potential of gridded cities, since one could see Monpazier as a miniature Manhattan; and comparison with the regular layouts of Winchelsea and Flint raised a pan-European vision. Later still, holidays in a house in Mérindol lent by Bobby Carter, one-time President of the AA, led to an investigation of the valley of the Durance, the market at Apt, the Roman remains at Saint-Rémy, the amphitheatre at Orange, the romantic ruins of Les Baux, and led finally to the discovery of Aix.

The special charm of Aix lies in its layout: the north half of it is Medieval and irregular, focused on a spacious market place in front of the Palais de Justice; the south half is a collection of aristocratic *hôtels particuliers*, laid out on a gridded plan in the seventeenth century, and it appears to have no centre, but just to be governed by a rule. The two districts are separated by a gracious boulevard, the Cours Mirabeau, also dating from the seventeenth century. It is shaded by enormous plane trees, and anchored at one end by a mossy fountain. The confrontation that results seemed to be that of inherited Tradition versus arbitrary Rule, and this no doubt helped to confirm the dialectical mental landscape which has dominated all my subsequent attempts at cultural criticism, the initial opposition of *Sweet Disorder and the Carefully Careless*. Or is it because my mind is ordered in duos that I like Aix?

On the seventeenth century side, there are virtually no shops, while the other side is lined with shops, bookstores, cafes and restaurants. Such a one-sided frontage would normally come about on a sea coast, as with Brighton or Nice, or facing a park, as with Princes Street in Edinburgh, a city with a similar dual layout. Here, what you are contemplating over there, while discussing your Campari-soda, is not strictly speaking a spectacle, but rather a kind of vacuity, formed by a nondescript combination of house facades and garden walls that enclose an unknown world of former privilege. There are connections: the cafe called Les Deux Garçons takes its name from the male caryatids that flank the doorway of the Hôtel d'Espagnet opposite, suggesting a sort of Mozartian refusal of any *droits du seigneur* that might remain. But the outlook towards that world of privilege has no focus, it is vague and diffuse, and the interest devolves instead on the parade, or passeggiata, that unfolds along the sidewalk, immediately in front. Because it is confined to a single sidewalk, it has a peculiar intensity. Rendezvous are given in the simple form of "*Cours Mirabeau, vers six heures*", so no one is quite sure where to find their friends, and all eyes are alert and searching.

And this situation is passionately interesting, since you are always about to discover a friend or acquaintance, or be discovered by one. This sense of expectation puts you on the *qui vive*, requires you to exercise a subtle assessment of character and style among the throng that passes. Some loved one is probably out there. While waiting, enjoy criticizing the tourists, self-consciously flaunting the discolouration of over-exposed limbs. In marked contrast is the studied insouciance of the natives, pursuing private goals in spite rather than because of the public gaze. There is the fascination afforded by groups, sometimes clearly constituting family relationships, sometimes marked by incongruity or eccentricity. Then there are rarer, but breathtaking, cases of individual expression, both male and female, where style is clearly the means and the motive for display. All this is upheld by the sense of Frenchness, that indefinable combination of ineffable chic and down-to-earth *bon sens*. And in the meantime, it appears that these enormous Campari-sodas have created that special kind of cultural imbalance that can only be resolved by a discriminating choice of restaurant for the evening meal. So, social Space has combined with Body to round out Life.

London, May 1997, published June 1997.

RM joins in a colloquium at POW School in Regent's Park on *Women in Architecture*, 4 June.

We go to the Royal Academy for Rem Koolhaas Lecture and reception, 7 June.

Julian and Teresa Scott throw a party at the Savile Club, 6 September.

Building Design asks for a review of Robin Evans' book.

TRANSLATIONS FROM DRAWING TO BUILDING, AND OTHER ESSAYS
REVIEW FOR *BUILDING DESIGN*
Robin Evans, Architectural Association Publications, 1997

I knew Robin Evans personally; he was always a very special person. But I have only just learned, through reading this book, that he could write. As a person, he had this special quality, a sort of inwardness. He was modest in demeanour, occasionally displaying scepticism or irony, but held his power in reserve. In his writing, his power erupts.

These essays have an amazing range, from cultural criticism through social studies to historical analysis and contemporary criticism. They are carried on a scholarship that is thorough and often painstaking without ever becoming an end in itself. They are not entertaining, or conversational, or prone to any kind of surface display. They seem to arrive directly from the author's puzzlement, and to be the result of his own effort to understand a problem and explain a situation to himself. As a result, he explains it for us. These reflections, apparently the result of his own search for peace of mind, become in themselves a source of new knowledge.

This strength is not built on withdrawal from events, but on an ability to rise above them. The first essay, "Towards Anarchitecture", speaks with the idealism of the 60s and anticipates a new freedom from oppressive social structures, engaging for example with the "over-rationalised supposition that social structure is a good thing to stabilise". The Archigram-type illustrations make more vivid the hopes of that moment to escape from the past. But the argument for creative mess rather than controlled neatness is not a projection of fantasy, however desirable, but comes from a sober assessment of the way action is produced through an excess of will over resistance, starting with his own perception that it is easier to get out of bed if the bedclothes are loose. The ability to personalise an abstract relation is one of the traits that, by revealing how his own thought arose, intensifies our interest in his argument.

He is always aware of the complexity of the social situation, which ideology attempts to simplify, and which for the individual, is accompanied by a similar complexity of motivation. He discusses a case where, for one individual, private adulation of a film star was a positive force for living a life. Could architecture—an anarchitecture—hope to find a link between public rule and private conduct?

Similar valid responses could conceivably be evoked by architecture. The
social has dissociated itself from this kind of charism-architectural logic
and, with incipient idiocy, has attached itself to another, the logic of
social manipulation…

That judgement of the rational phase of Modernism, with its nascent perspicacity balanced by "incipient idiocy", is typical of the way that Evans surprises us while handing us a discovery.

The work that Evans has done on rationalist strategies applied in prison and workhouse has already established his reputation as a critic perceptive of the links between physical structures and moral ideologies. Essays in this collection on the walled enclave and on Housing Reform confirm this reputation. Altogether more riveting is his analogy between the way figures fill a painting by Raphael to the exclusion of the background, and the way people of that time filled the spaces of their buildings, where all the spaces were directly linked. The invention of the corridor, then, becomes another instrument for analysing and controlling the social scene. He shows how this drive to analyse activities and control them permeates the first stages of Modernism in architecture.

The essays on "Translations from Drawing to Buildings", and on "The Developed Surface", could only have been written by an architect. Yet the lessons he draws out are far from being merely technical, but reach out to the lived experience of architecture with its power to modify both what the drawing may reveal and what it may conceal. In the case of Philibert de l'Orme's design for the tracery in the dome of the Royal Chapel at Anet, he shows how the architect used subterfuge in explaining his methodology, with the aim of creating a perfect reflection between the dome's pattern and that of the floor—both however being subtly divergent and imperfect. This is another case of closely observed planes.

The essays in straight architectural criticism, on "Eisenman's Fin d'Ou T Hou S" and Mies' "Barcelona Pavilion", show a masterly appreciation of intentions that diverge far, far from the assumed norm of quietly following function. In both cases, the critic gets close to the centre of the labyrinth and confronts the beast—the secret will of the architect to follow his vision, whatever myth may be erected in justification. As he exits, we have the feeling that the myth, in both cases, was a mere screen for an exploration of ambiguous feelings.

This writing is serious and unpretentious. It is leavened by wit and percipience. There is an ability to concentrate on essentials and pay attention to the evidence, that commands our respect and gains our interest. And the sheer originality of the thought it encloses only increases the sense of the loss we have suffered by his untimely death.

London, June 1997.

Valerie Eliot visits Mall Studios to inspect Celia's bust of TS Eliot: she approves, 23 July.

B gives lunch at Bertorelli's to Ria Stein, agent for Birkhauser publisher, 18 August.

A trip to Paris: Hotel de Nevers: meet Martin at La Rotonde, see Brancusi, 26/29 August.

Harvard Design Magazine asks for a piece on *Durability*, which gives subject for thought, was interesting to write. But they don't publish it.

DURABILITY
ESSAY OFFERED TO *THE HARVARD DESIGN MAGAZINE*

The monument is made to endure, but not as the full presence of the one whose memory it bears; this, on the contrary, remains only as a memory. The techniques of art, for example, and perhaps above all else poetic versification, can be seen as stratagems—which themselves are, not coincidentally, minutely institutionalised and monumentalised—that transform the work of art into a residue and into a monument capable of enduring because from the outset it is produced in the form of that which is dead. It is capable of enduring not because of its force, but because of its weakness. [1]

Gianni Vattimo

At an early age I read Pierre Loti on the Easter Island heads, which were created in mystery and have endured long after the people who raised them have disappeared. If we try to imagine a society painfully carving and erecting these heads, for whatever mysterious purpose, we have to assume that those people had a life, that they cooked and ate and possessed pots and pans, shelter and hearth, buildings probably, even if made of fragile material. All has vanished that was not endurable, and the stone heads that remain no longer figure in living memories, except those of the tourists, for whom they are a mystery and have no precise meaning. In a sense the heads too have vanished, along with the islanders, since they no longer define an essence in the collective memory, since they no longer make sense.

It remains a matter of speculation why these enormous stone heads were so important, what role they fulfilled in the social structure, what sacrifice they entailed, what reassurance they provided, why so many were needed, why it was always good to put up one more. The very number of them in itself suggests that they were in some practical way viewed as efficacious, perhaps not as monuments so much as instruments of survival. In an array of objects of utility that might have been commonly in use, such as palm-frond roofs, wooden posts, woven aprons, leather sandals, fibre thongs, stone hearths, the stone outlasted all other materials, in the end outlasted the society itself. The place of stone in that society may have approached the meaning of eternity in religious systems, and it would be useless to speculate if this was a primary case of durable figures coming to stand for an afterlife, or if the final failure of the Easter Island ecology was anticipated by several generations, implying that the stones were raised ultimately through despair.

The material hierarchy whereby stone was important because it was durable, as gold was durable, represents a pre-semiological state of society, where meanings were not fleeting or metaphoric, but literal and self-evident; where symbolism, though practised, existed at the very fringe of the unconscious. Gold was also rare, or rare enough, to be special; and the very durability of stone was matched by the difficulty of working it and raising it, so that it absorbed human energy and became imbued with effort and value.

A change is presaged by the expansion of consciousness that followed the Copernican revolution. If Palladio could offer, in place of stone columns, brick columns cased in stucco, Western society had already reached a stage where form had overtaken substance. How much had already been lost since Dante! In Renaissance poetry, form meant substance.[2] Language was a surface that unequivocally expressed a hidden truth. Today, truth must be invented as we skid along on the surface. Substance slips from our grasp, eludes us except as memory.

Stone once stood for forever, and seemed to stand forever. Today it crumbles and spalls in the polluted atmosphere. The Parthenon will be better preserved as fragments in an air-conditioned museum, bereft of meaning. Buildings are designed for a limited lifespan, and are often replaced before this has elapsed. Even buildings only recently completed are torn down to make way for more remunerative facilities. The building, conceived as a monument to endure, is already overtaken by its value as a text, to be memorised. At the same time, photographic records are proliferating, so that the record of what once existed on the ground has become multiple, and itself a source of confusion. We have entered the age of the infinite library, as anticipated by Borges. Books are not as durable as stone, and the proliferation of books represents a retreat from simple durability into something else. Then a further step, the metamorphosis of the printed word into computer memory banks, carries proliferation beyond reckoning.

Our age is characterised by its lack of definition, its retreat from the material into the mental, from the actual into the virtual. Objects no longer shine with an inner life, they exist only to the extent that they are the same as, or different from, other objects, and so to the extent that they are imprinted by the system. They have a multiple and insecure existence, accompanied by the blurring of images and the overlapping of memories. History becomes a collection of specialisations no longer capable of being integrated into a master narrative, so it loses its simplicity and its narrative power. Faced with the complexity of the actual, History becomes untellable. The act of writing, the exercise of art, take on the character of an introspective activity performed within a personal memory stocked with discarded fragments, a solipsistic exercise in personal mnemonics, a sort of burrowing in the junk pile. More respectably, it can be seen as an individual act of animating the collective archive. But then, does the archive exist, outside of the collection of individual memories?

But if even stone is not durable enough, are we not at an advantage through our very ability to recognise this? The conditions of life were once thought to resemble a narrative: the biblical story of Jesus of Nazareth or a fairy story like "Jack the Giant-

Killer" are equally credible when narrative has the power to unfold a life. If the story was incomplete, the invention of an afterlife was the logical way to achieve completion. Now no one knows what plot is unfolding, no one is in the position of the storyteller, we can only vaguely imagine a narrative that enfolds life. Our life is not being told by us. But if that is where language and consciousness have brought us to, is it not as well to recognise this? Are we not strong, through our very weakness?

The religious spirit that sees God as Providence faces a problem every time populations are overwhelmed by earthquake or flood, resulting in the destruction of the innocent along with the guilty, and making impossible a theory of religion as retribution and reward. Voltaire exposed this problem in his discussion of the Lisbon earthquake, and insisted that chance is chance and not destiny. That in a way sums up modernity. Chance and complexity together destroy the narrative, along with the values that entered it. Yet we are discontent with the loss of meaning, meaning is what we desire to recuperate.

As for the architect, he hesitates to abandon the power of material in its materiality. Building as idea cannot be allowed to float free from its limitations, except at the risk of becoming a mere text. In search of recuperating meaning, a material basis must be found. The equivalent of stone has become metal, no longer valued for its endurance but for its particularity in combination with its plasticity. Metal can be bent, melted, cast, reworked, lost and found; it permits of multiple futures, and yet holds us firmly in our chronological tracks, bound to the future as other societies were bound to the past. The monument as a statement in memoriam has been replaced with the machine as an instrument of survival. Norberg-Schulz, discussing Kahn (and making use of Heidegger) notes that he oscillates between facticity and the as-yet-uncovered. We need not be caught within this either-or, says Andrew Benjamin. Building must be conceived as practice, carried along on unknown conditions, rather than as the result of applying already-defined rules.[3]

It is clear that 'already-defined rules' are inadequate in the face of an indefinite future. They risk being destroyed by new conditions they are ill placed to anticipate. In place of rules, we are to prefer laws—the laws of Nature—that are supposedly part of the universe out there rather than of the doomed subject in here, that is to say, they are unchanging. But is this desire for indefinite adaptability not the residue of the desire for certainty upon which societies were formerly based, before modernity? It is as if we could not conceive of putting ourselves at a loss, of losing face, of having to revise our rules. There is to be no lament, no search for a lost essence, but rather a return to the arbitrariness of time. It is futile to seek to express the sense of loss as a form of social healing, for to efface the need is to sacrifice the hope of a new resolution.

That would be, in my own terms, to undervalue the sense of the tragic, through which alone the human condition can come to terms with its unknown destiny. The tragic requires that we mourn the loss, but seek always to overcome it by a fresh effort. Our culture has no hope of establishing a future as a comfortable part of the unchanging laws of nature, substituting the unknown future, to which we are already reconciled, for what was formerly conceived of as eternal life. The laws of Nature suggest that our ecology will come to an end as surely as did that of the Easter Islanders, and human culture will vanish, removing all meaning from material objects, stone or metal. In the meantime, we exist in a flux, but with certain mental needs that exceed the limitations and the arbitrariness of time.

Gianni Vattimo is right to conclude that the techniques of art are the stratagems that transform the work of art into a residue, and so into a monument capable of enduring. To endure, architecture also must emulate poetic versification, searching out that narrow space between technique and form, from which meaning emerges. Every medium contains this space, it is only necessary to realise the medium, whatever its proper materials, as the container of the space of the poetic. Hear what emanates from this space, however distant already is the moment when it was imprisoned there:

> *Not without wonder, not without delight*
> *Mine eyes have viewed, in contemplation's depth*
> *This work of wit, divine and excellent.*
> *What shape, what substance, or what unknown power*
> *In virgin's habit, crowned with laurel leaves*
> *And olive branches woven in between*
> *On sea-girt rocks, like to a goddess shines?*
> *O front! O face! O all celestial, sure,*
> *And more than mortal.*

From Ben Jonson (1573–1637), "Cynthia's Revels"

London, July 1997.

1. Vattimo, Gianni, *The End of Modernity*, trans. Jon R Snyder, Oxford: Blackwell, 1988, p. 86.
2. Williams, Raymond, *Keywords*, Glasgow: Fontana, Collins, 1976, p. 113.
3. Benjamin, Andrew, in a lecture at the Architectural Association, London, 26 February 1996.

RM visits *The Priory* in Hampstead: swimming pool in basement has clear view up to sky, 13 October.

The client, asked how she manages to live in minimalist space, says that when someone calls, everything is thrown into the cupboards.

We visit the open-air sculpture gallery at Ockley in Surrey; lunch at the Red Lion, 18 October.

RM publishes *Enlightenment: a villa in Hampstead by Rick Mather Architects*, RIBA Journal.

ENLIGHTENMENT: A VILLA IN HAMPSTEAD BY RICK MATHER ARCHITECTS
REVIEW IN *RIBA JOURNAL*

This is a white-walled villa in the classical tradition: modern, but orderly. Seeking it, there is no doubt when one has found it, it has a presence: a good deal of calm white wall, with limited openings judiciously placed; a corner window without glazing bars or corner mullion. The horizontal plate glass porch roof and vertical roof terrace screens give a hint of power in reserve, but there is nothing roguish about the effect. Seen from the road it presents a modest two-storey mass, set back a full house width from the street, screened by a high wall and fence. To the rear, the three-storey garden side towards the falling ground is virtually invisible. Externally it suits its environment perfectly: there are plenty of other white walls in this area, some are modern villas, even famous ones, and some are Arts and Crafts *fin-de-siècle* romantic houses: no cause for alarm.

Internally, it is sensational, altogether not your ordinary interior: sensational in effect, and sensational because it engages actively with the senses. There is a swimming pool in the lowest floor, and its presence is evident from all the other levels because the living room floor incorporates at key points windows that allow you to look down on it. I say windows, but they are transparent sections of the floor that can be walked upon if you are feeling strong. Some parts of the house have voids that extend right up to the roof, so there is a play of space. Above all, because of the pool, there is a play of light. At the time of my visit we were under the regime of the standard overcast northern sky, but there was still this sense of light coming at you from all sides. In brilliant sunlight, the effect will be spectacular.

This is Modernism in the tradition of Modernism, owing a debt to the classic villas of Le Corbusier. Although horizontal sheets of plate glass are used to seal off the immediate pool environment, the space rises vertically from the lowest to the highest levels. The flow of space through all three storeys creates a sense of sculptural intention. The space gradient runs downhill from the entrance on the middle level to the garden outlet at the far end of the pool, but this frontality is countered by the movement at right angles that flows from the study area on the top floor down to the garden terrace outside the dining room, which is further emphasised by the main window—a roof light facing south and protected by an external blind—that again restates the historical link with the artists' studios of Paris that first ventured into big windows. But the combination of two space gradients crossing each other already expresses an evolved concept of space, more complex than we find anywhere in Le Corbusier. To this we must add a different, less classical, sense of materiality: the use of glass, whether horizontal or vertical, whether transparent or mirrored, creates a sort of blur, an uncertainty about limits that makes the final outcome very different from the inherited models.

There is a very Corbusian moment when we stand on the little balcony off the study area and look back into the body of the house. From this point the spatial composition opens up in all directions, and one is positively glad of the anchor provided by the blank panel that screens the bedroom corridor directly opposite. This projects into the well (to provide cupboard space in the corridor) as a singularity, in a way highly reminiscent of the way the roof terrace projects into the upper part of the living room in the Maison Cook, 1926, by way of a segmental blank wall. In both cases, a sculptural mass works to stabilise spatial flow.

Nowhere in Le Corbusier do we find the play of narrow slots of glazing introduced to clarify the massing and the limits of the masses. This is more to do with postmodern angst and the search for conceptual clarity. For example the projection that encloses the entrance hall at ground level, and the shower room above it, is separated from the main volume by such a slot, requiring that the bather passes through a visible zone before reaching the privacy of the shower. It's no surprise to find that the owner has insisted on this glass being etched. (Did Peter Eisenman run into similar problems with his House 5, one wonders.) Yet the slot still works to make one aware of the spatial hierarchy.

The aesthetic effect is further de-stabilised by the play of light, whether directly entering or reflected upward from the pool. The upper edges of the plate-glass balcony fronts slice into the air, threatening as well as reassuring, blurring contours with their reflections while defining them with surgical precision. The glass treads to all the stairs draw attention to our movement as a poetic, sculptural promenade rather than as a practical motion. What will it be like when these conditions have become so familiar that one can run downstairs two steps at a time? But perhaps the advent of the mobile phone makes all such hurrying obsolete.

Even without sun glitter, even when all is still, the horizontal planes of glass and the pool itself create diagonals by means of the reflections they produce of the stairs, suggesting an Escher-like ambiguity, recreating a hunger for n-dimensional geometry, the desire to escape from gravity, an invocation perhaps of Lissitzky's call for "floating structures", his anticipation of a "physical-dynamic architecture" requiring "the conquest of gravity". This is part of today's climate, our wish to extend from real limits into artificial ones that we ourselves choose, like the desire for cyberspace.

If these remarks lean towards formal criticism, this is not to suggest that the architect has floated away from his task. He was chosen out of five architects interviewed, and his sketch solution to a complex brief was instantly accepted. The client clearly wanted a house that would go beyond mere convenience and become in its own right a work of art. At the same time it is laid out with a great practicality, for example in separating the two single bed-studies into corners in the ground floor where they are virtually removed from the spatial drama of the main house, so making them good for guests or grandchildren. It is wonderfully sensitive to the immediate outside prospect, so that the main windows are directed at the best and most idyllic views, and the walls as well as moulding a dynamic space also hide the adjacent buildings. In this respect the building is an object lesson in showing what is lost by the Miesian approach of opening up all the elevations on all sides, how more convincing screening by wall is to screening by flimsy venetian blinds. In addition, the space of corridors and cupboards is on an ample scale, allowing on occasion a swift transition from domestic squalor to pristine display.

By eschewing the provision of covered garages, the front and back gardens are made into coherent spaces that define the domain of the villa, giving a paved herb garden on the public side and a classic lawn-under-trees on the other. There is a generous provision of sitting out space adjacent to all the main functions, so that the outside is immediately available whenever the sun shines. From the lawn, the southwest elevation is an end in itself: stabilised by the recess where the pool reaches the outside, activated by the asymmetrical play between the remaining windows. It fulfils in ampler form the promise of the entrance side.

The house is full of light, but from all sides, competing in a complex and enjoyable dance: a great place to live, and an impressive piece of architecture.

London, October 1997, published November 1997.

ECSTATIC SPACE
ROYAL ACADEMY

The ecstatic is not an everyday experience, it doesn't happen on the number 24 bus. It has to be prepared, and it corresponds to a delicate state of mind. For me it occurs when the mind has been elevated to a certain level, when it is full of aspiration and expectation, and one way of achieving that condition is through the contemplation of high art. It's not necessary to be literally high, but to be somehow off the ground.

This experience came to me in its most definitive form during a visit to the church of San Carlino alle Quattro Fontane, in Rome—a long-standing enthusiasm, always the first thing to visit when in Rome. One had read Portoghesi, one had already been elevated by the masterly simplicity of Borromini's concept. The oval figure of plan and dome has a primacy as formal invention, as if the whole building were unfolding the consequences of a single fundamental axiom. The longer axis of the oval has been melded with the long axis of the Medieval church to make something entirely new. As Portoghesi says, the long dimension has been squeezed to form the short dimension, or is it the short dimension that has been extended to form the long dimension? The space fluctuates, the building breathes.

Then the elaboration of apses, one on each of the four axial points, is enough to confuse the initial idea, and introduce a perplexing complexity. The distribution of the pilasters is by groups of four, the outside pair belonging to two adjoining groups, so that the fours can be read in two different ways: as definition of the apsidal emphasis, or as a counter emphasis on the diagonals. The space is an articulation of four concavities, or it is an articulation of four convexities, or it is both, if you can stretch your mind to embrace the contradiction. The orders, the apsidal half-domes with their reticulated ceilings, the dome balanced on four circles with its complicated pattern of noughts and crosses, all combine to direct the eyes upward towards the eye of the dome in the classic posture of aspiration and awe. And then, you see the cornice.

This church is a Baroque masterpiece, and one is used to the high-handed Baroque way with the orders, by which, generally, the columns no longer enclose static aediculae, each one a pause point of contemplation, but rather keep the eye moving upwards to the climax, breaking out through the horizontal bandings to create an upwards surge, dynamic like Gothic shafts. But here, there are no breaks in the cornice where the columns reach it:

San Carlino alle Quattro Fontane,
interior towards altar
Borromini, 1667

San Carlino alle Quattro Fontane,
detail of cornice
Borromini

it continues on its horizontal sweep of the church without a pause. So it delineates the basic form of the church as four apsidal recesses combining to make a unity. The only deviation in the continuity of the cornice is the shallow angle where it passes from one recess to the next, from one curve to the next. The cornice moves horizontally, and it moves fast; it never stops, and, for me, it counters the complexity of the classical order with an almost streamlined simplicity: it makes Borromini a Modern.

Following the cornice with the eyes one is soon dizzy. Within the complexities of the Baroque it makes a moment of breathtaking simplicity. In the atmosphere of high religious sentiment, it asserts a moment of sheer physicality, bringing us close to the erotic. We have reached the ecstatic.

Could we go on from this to attempt a definition of the ecstatic? If it represents some intrusion of a physical immediacy in a scene of otherworldly contemplation, it must happen wherever those conditions hold good. As, for instance, with the swooning ecstasy of Bernini's Saint Teresa in Santa Maria della Vittoria, Rome, where the naked angel appears to the saint with all the potency of a visitation, and the immediacy of a sexual encounter. But, within architecture, things cannot be done quite so directly, the abstract must be involved. Interesting to note that when Borromini does a very similar thing with the cornice in the interior of Sant'Ivo, Rome, it doesn't produce the same effect, because the massiveness of the pilasters and the right angles they engender kill the speed of the cornice. But a very similar effect does occur with Guarini's dome at the Cathedral of SS Sindone in Turin, where a succession of fanlights, each course spanning between the apices of the ones below, creates a primitive effect like a game of child's building blocks, which at the same time builds the form of an intricate dome that shimmers with an unearthly light. The contrast between primitive means and transcendental goal reaches close to the ecstatic.

These examples derive from a religious setting, where a devotional atmosphere survives an intervention that is physical in its brutality. It's hard to imagine that modern design could do anything similar. Yet there may be a parallel condition, even if the meanings have altered. One remembers the shimmering intricacy of the high roof in Foster's Sainsbury Centre at the University of East Anglia. In that case everything is revealed, and everything is physical—structural lattices, service pipes, lighting runs, louvres: they combine to form a decor where it is the total effect that rules. Where the means are physical, because functional, there can still be a cumulative effect that transcends the functional: but there is no element of shock, or intervention.

International Terminal, Waterloo, View from outside
Nicholas Grimshaw, 1993

International Terminal, Waterloo, View inside
Nicholas Grimshaw

Perhaps there has to be something more like a contradiction: if modern functionalism can produce magic by transcending the merely functional, but moves always in a single direction towards fulfilment, we need an intervention that reverses that direction and undermines the devotional atmosphere. Our architecture is not ostensibly built on metaphor, as was the case in the classical era, but is only obliquely metaphorical, and ostensibly and irremediably physical. So with us, a merely physical intervention would not prick the bubble of belief. But wait, we are material girls and boys, but we do believe in the physical. In our age, the High-Tech does produce a certain devotional aura, because it is a system that passes from the gratification of needs to the fulfilment of beliefs—an entirely ideological system in which is inscribed the worship of technology as the great provider, and of science as the power of the future. So an intervention would have to signal an abrupt abandonment of that quasi-rational system of belief.

I do find something magical in the way Nicholas Grimshaw has managed the vault over the Channel Tunnel Terminus at Waterloo. And he is an architect who believes in the craft of construction to a positively Ruskinian degree, loving it every minute. Viewed from the outside, it's clear that the lattice structure simply moves from the underside to the outside of the glazing, about a third of the way across, at the hinge point of the portal arch. Viewed from within the space, it's as if the structure disappeared before its job was done. The result has something supernatural, recalling the power of a great cantilever projecting from one side only. What it involves, in terms of our hypothesis, is not the sudden intrusion of a physical reality, but its sudden disappearance, making a mystery where all before was plain. The rational system has been contradicted, apparently, by an arbitrary but inspired intervention. Allied with the long curve of the vault, it gets close to the ecstatic for me.

London, December 1997.

1998

RM goes to Tokyo for the RA and British Council. He lectures on *British Architecture from the Pacific Rim*, *British Architecture Symposium New Urban Environments*, Laforet Museum, Tokyo 21 to 25 January.

Published: James Stirling, *Writings on Architecture*, with introduction by RM, Milan: Skira Editore, 1988.

RM introduces Rick Mather for his lecture at the Building Centre, 18 February.

We attend the RIBA for Ed and Jeremy's presentation of their work, and dinner, 5 March.

RM appears in court at Stevenage, and is fined for speeding on the way to Mary Banham's new house; licence endorsed, but no points given, 18 March.

We go to Barcelona, where RM is due to lecture on Stirling; we visit the studio of Miralles and chat to him, April.

Miralles warns of pickpockets, yet a few moments later, RM succumbs to a gypsy woman pinning a rose on his breast. All our travel money gone!

B gives seminar, *Almost Nothing*, on the Barcelona Pavilion, for Carles Muro at AA, 18 May.

We go to Charles Jencks' birthday Ball on the roof at Derry and Tom's, 25 May

Lecture: *The Truth About Myth*, in a Symposium on the High-Tech, Royal Academy, June.

THE TRUTH ABOUT THE MYTH
SYMPOSIUM ON THE HIGH-TECH AT THE ROYAL ACADEMY

The actual exponents of what most of us call the High-Tech style are not in agreement that what they do has anything to do with style. Nick Grimshaw has insisted that his architecture is mainly about putting materials together with respect, and even love—he wants to be a sort of latter-day follower of Ruskin. Norman Foster insists that his concerns are to do with people, the architect should be primarily an enabler. Richard Rogers, in explaining the aims of his team in designing the Pompidou Centre, insisted that it was all about change and adaptability:

> *We want our building to be adapted and changed by the people who use it, we want to stop the architecture being a straitjacket, inhibiting ideas. We want the outside to reflect the activities inside, and we want to encourage the maximum possible participation by the public with the specialist users and the things on display.*

This insider's view suggests that the reason why High-Tech is not a style to those who can do it is that for them a building should, in principle, be a mere mechanism for human desires and activities. It should not obtrude itself between desire and fulfilment, it should not be an end in itself. It should be transparent.

The architect who has most consistently followed this line must be Cedric Price, who has consented to and even encouraged the demolition of his Interactive Centre in Camden, and opposed those who would now like to list it as a monument to expendable architecture. In pursuit of the transparent, in love with the diagram, Cedric has approached invisibility.

Whether High-Tech is a style or not seems to depend on whether we see it from inside or outside. The insider sees it as a technique that goes directly to the needs of the client and puts no obstacle to their realisation. The outsider sees a series of obsessive artefacts that, in the words of the poet Robert Herrick, are too precise in every part. They present the image of the machine, gleaming, precise, powerful.

This is the final version of the modern style, the culmination of the functionalism of the machine aesthetic that originated around 1910 with Mies, Behrens and Le Corbusier. It was not intended to be a style, but it became one because it produced artefacts of a consistent character, and this consistency in the end filled a space and had to be named. In our *fin-de-siècle* it represents the last stage of the vision that architecture could shed all secondary attributes and concentrate on essentials. And Grimshaw has named those essentials as Structure, Space and Skin.

This invariable outcome may not be the result of following a style, but it must be the result of something invariable, an invariable attitude, I would suggest, and this attitude is best characterised as Naturalism. What we perceive as the High-Tech style is the consequence of believing that the building can be transparent to life, so that it reveals life as it is, or at least as it wants to be. There is an idealism at work here, the belief that functionalism is not an -ism, but really works.

Ideal structures are the rowing racer, the glider, where concentration on the physical performance of materials under stress produce a naked structure that appears to owe everything to science and nothing to culture. Science deals with the forces of nature, and so should architecture. The shell is an ideal structure that is an acute combination of structure, skin and living space, and the architect of the shell is nature. This is the same philosophy of design that emanated from D'Arcy Thompson's seminal book *On Growth and Form*, which became the architect's bible in the England of 1937.

In the act of building, it is the structure that provides the basic framework, and that both symbolises, and is, necessity. Most High-Tech buildings expose their structure as the essential aspect of their nature, and in doing so, celebrate the structure as an aspect of truth. Structures made of steel and glass were from the beginning of the Modern Movement considered the most direct expression of modernity, combining the twin aspects of functionalism: the structure stripped down to the bones and made visible, space freed by the transparency.

But there are certain practical aspects of building that militate against this clarity. In the Centre Pompidou, for instance, the basic structure must be protected against fire, and the cheapest way to do this is to spray the steel with a protective material. At the end of this operation, the steel cage looks like a chicken loft. To restore the smooth surface that goes with technical precision, the structure has to be further encased in another sleeve, usually a casing of light metal in aluminium or stainless steel. This a complex operation, neither cheap to carry out nor aesthetically consonant with exposing an underlying reality. It is not a stripping down, but a building up. The structure you see is not the naked steel, but an elegant sheathing that is thicker and more monumental than the actual structure which it protects. So a sophisticated High-Tech building is rarely the most direct result of practical necessity, but an elaborate artifice that speaks, often eloquently, of a necessity that has been invented.

The reason the Pompidou has so much structure is that the architects wanted to have large floor spaces uninterrupted by structural columns, so that the building could be said to be flexible—that is, ready for unforeseen possibilities of use—and also "free" at a symbolic level. Every single beam has to be a deep lattice girder—a form usually adopted for engineering structures like bridges. A column-free floor would indeed be very useful if it was desired to install an ice hockey rink or a dodgem car fairground. So far such uses have not proved necessary for the Pompidou to fulfill its function as library and art gallery. So in the interest of pure possibilities the structure has been greatly inflated, making it monumental and heroic in scale. Both structure and space combine to declare an ideological commitment.

This does not arise out of any inadequacy on the part of the architects, but out of a desire to reach out to the future. It is precisely this desire that lifts the building into the realm of rhetoric and sustains the mythic aspect of its modernity. People have responded in due measure, and the building has been immensely popular, thereby no doubt justifying its expense, far beyond what strict cost accounting would have allowed. Thus, for function to exist as a myth, it has to be made larger than life and given the strangeness of things still to come. It points to a mythic future, beckons to utopia.

At the same time, it has a familiar aspect, it has become a popular myth. It speaks in the name of truth to nature, it is free from the personal whim of an architect with aspirations to high art. It is thought of as a style independent from the vagaries of the architect, a style that can be guaranteed to deliver the goods, free from the perils of introspection, free from personal prejudice. Does this not explain why the High-Tech 'style' has been such a potent factor in recent British architecture? Is it possible that the corridors of power are still running on the assumption that architecture that looks like engineering is least likely to conceal a personal vision?

Far from following a path of least resistance in pursuing purely functional requirements, it has, from the beginning attempted to project a highly ideological belief in the power of science and technology, as the only sure way of anticipating the future and achieving power in architecture. Far from being matter-of-fact in its approach, it has reflected an underlying romanticism about life and living, in the tradition of English landscape architecture, which looks natural, but is indeed highly artificial.

On this reading, it is not odd that some such style should surface in Britain rather than in the United States, where landscape simply imitates the wilderness, or rejects it. Here the wilderness must be civilised and absorbed into culture as an amenity, yet made to look as if it happened naturally. The stroll around the park is agreeable and no threat to young ladies, yet skirts the improper as it passes the Temple of Love or the Grotto. This flirtation with sweet disorder can be taken to represent a continuity in the British pursuit of happiness.

It is true that exponents of the High-Tech (let me call it) approach have been changing along with everything else. It seems that change is hardly something the architect must strive to accommodate, but something that overtakes us all. As the century rolls to a close Nick Grimshaw is happy to disclose that his clients have come to demand "something else".

> *... clients have come to perceive that what is justified in the name of order, economy and geometry is governed also by other forces. We now have clients who expect architecture to be an art and to have creative force behind it.*

London, December 1997.

Trip to France, stay in Spencer de Grey's house at Geay; fine supper on boat to St-Malo, to 17 July.

On first day RM springs a tendon (his Achilles heel), jumping off a zebra crossing, is hobbling for rest of stay.

We are wowed by hundreds and hundreds of hollyhocks in the seaside churchyard at Talmont.

Daphne Portway falls over dead while playing tennis. To comfort her, Celia goes to Eleanor at Cambridge, 31 July.

We attend Daphne's funeral service in the chapel of St Catherine's College, 7 August.

RM publishes *The Work of Stirling-Wilford* for Birkhauser Verlag, Artemis Series.

RM takes his granddaughter Lucy May for a day out at the Science Museum, she presses every button in sight, and twice 'loses' him, deliberately, so exhausting him. For lunch she chooses sausage and mash: "Why? I know about it, we get it at school", 8 September.

Phaidon book launch at the Coq d'Argent, No.1 Poultry, we go along, 17 September.

NO.1 POULTRY
REVIEW FOR *THE ARCHITECT'S JOURNAL*

This building is a monument to Peter Palumbo, and to his determination to bring a building of distinction to the City of London. It took some 23 years of controversy and a full-scale public enquiry before the Secretary of State finally rejected the Miesian design and Palumbo finally gave up hopes for a Miesian masterpiece. By then Mies himself was dead.

It was in July 1985 that Palumbo turned to James Stirling for something that the city would accept. Dozens of architects would have shown exemplary promptitude in fulfilling such a valuable commission. But Stirling was no facile postmodernist. He had his own agenda, and he stirred a fresh controversy. It has taken another 13 years and a second public enquiry for Stirling's design to be accepted and built. By now Stirling himself is dead.

Many will say it is at least 13 years out of date, that postmodernism has had its day, luckily short-lived, that a building so clearly monumental is politically incorrect, that a monument finished in striped stone is an anachronism in an age of transparency and openness. Such reactions illustrate the shallowness of political ideology. In another few years buildings will probably be criticised for not obviously expressing their purpose—a shipping office should look like a ship, an art gallery should look like modern art, and so on. A new Expressionism is taking over. Anything else is old hat.

And anything opaque is clearly an object, to be avoided in an age of process, and a monument, to be avoided in an age of instant death, death being now as meaningless as a zapp. It is 60 years since Lewis Mumford wrote "The Death of the Monument", an essay included in *Circle* of 1937, that strangely circumspect celebration of the coming of abstract art to Britain. But Poultry is both abstract and representational, in a way not possible to the architect of that time.

We British are obsessed with good form, with doing what is proper. We think always of what is the right thing to do, the question of what, and we hardly pay attention at all to the question of how, the exploration of feeling, uniqueness and newness, the boundary of other possibilities where art assumes the power of spiritual renewal. Be glad therefore that we have a character as obdurate and as insightful as Peter Palumbo, and that the City of London has against all the odds almost certainly acquired a masterpiece.

Stirling was always strangely open to 'other' ways; soft with students, tolerant of ideas thrown up in his office, tolerant even of his critics. What interests us in his work is not its political correctness, but the unexpected qualities that it uncovers. He believed in function, of course—he was a man of his age—but he also believed that architecture is an art. As art, it must exceed its utility, and reveal new strangeness.

This is a City building, exaggeratedly dressed in stone and rich in compositional plays, taking its place in a collection of rule-bound buildings; contextual, too, in responding to a neighbourhood of triangular sites. The prow is parodic of the rule-bound Mappin & Webb it replaces. The mood is irreverent, not respectful. There is a gleeful enjoyment of observing the rules and at the same time sending them up. At one level the building stands for the common citizen taking over the privileged realm of business. The central core—a cylinder open to the sky—is a sister of the hollow core at the Staatsgalerie, and it is open also as a short cut, or to access the tube station. Shortly, when the pub opens, it will be possible to put down a Guinness in full view of one of Stirling's squat conical capitals (at the southwest corner). In this it is robustly democratic. It increases cheerfulness in a more earthy way than transparency.

But it also rewards in more subtle ways. For the architect it is an object lesson in the shoehorning of separate functions into a tight space. The core cylinder is invaded by triangles of office accommodation so that the requisite office area is obtained without sacrificing the geometry. The triangular wells that open the basement to the view of the sky follow an exacting pattern of alternance. The entrances occur at significant points, without obstructing the sense of public place. The VIP entrance at the prow is there and not-there until required, and the amazing tunnel that links it to the upper piazza is an essay in pure 'architecturality', passing through contours that decorate its vault without introducing a single arbitrary note. This architecturality is achieved without pomp and ceremony. But this is not to say that it does not hold also a genuine sense of the tragic dimension that makes cheerfulness a duty as well as an enjoyment. Rowan Moore expressed this when he noticed the shadow of the mausoleum and the sense of geological time. For all its cheekiness, it is a serious piece of architecture. It holds up superbly in a confluence of famous buildings by Lutyens, Cooper, Dance and Soane, a city building at a meeting of city streets, modern, classical and romantic all at once.

Perhaps most enjoyable, from the way it expresses the exhilaration of invading a privileged realm and taking it over, is the roof garden. Thanks to the collaboration of landscapist Arabella Lennox-Boyd, it provides two distinct fantasies: a Ledouvian formality at the tip, and a Piranesian wilderness around the core. Small wonder that another sagacious wit has been quick to acquire this site as a setting for his own brand of *détente*—Conran at the Coq d'Argent. The clean geometry and the superb detailing also testify to the generosity with which Michael Wilford and his partners have absorbed and redeployed the Stirling spirit and carried the game through with zest.

London, 14 September 1998, published 5 November 1998.

RM delivers first Christopher Dean Memorial lecture at AA: *A Distant View of the Modern Movement*, 24 September.

Trip to Oxford for Rowe party, we put up at the Eastgate Hotel; visit Rousham, 3/4 October.

B and C to Dundee: lecture: *Stirling's Theory* for Dundee University, stay near Michael Spens. 5/6 November.

We go to Cambridge, C takes E to crematorium. Daphne Memorial in Newham Chapel, 20/22 November.

RIBA awards Royal Gold Medal to Oscar Niemeyer, in ceremony at Rio, because he won't fly: RM writes the citation.

RM contributes to the *Encyclopaedia of Architecture of the 20th Century*, Hatje Verlag, Stuttgart.

RM contributes his Tokyo speech to *British Architecture and the Urban Environment* for Royal Academy-Prestel.

1999

To Pina Bausch at Sadlers Wells: Viktor: Wonderful, 30 January.

To Cornwall for John and Su's birthday celebration: river barbecue.

At interval, B plays keyboard in band. 19/21 February.

B introduces Charles Jencks for his lecture to Twentieth Century Society at Cowcross Street, 4 March.

Lecture: *Can the Tragic Appear in Architecture?* in a colloquium, Royal Academy, 16 March.

APPROACHING THE VOID:
CAN THE TRAGIC APPEAR IN ARCHITECTURE?
PRESENTATION FOR THE ROYAL ACADEMY SYMPOSIUM

The symposium on Minimalism was an attempt to explore the limits of expression. By eliminating almost everything, by leaving almost nothing, could we begin to sense what are the essentials? A similar theme preoccupies us today. Can art approach the unspeakable? Can it engender a sense of the limits of life and of human understanding? Can it approach the tragic? And if art can do so, can architecture do so also?

The tragic demands death, the event on which there is no going back. But it is not simply the fact of death, but its impact in a defined poetic context. The multiplication of death does not induce the tragic. The Black Death, the Potato Famine, the daily earthquake, are, simply, calamities. The "tragic death" of Baby William, shaken to death by his au pair, is sad indeed, but not by itself tragic. Tragedy and comedy are genres, initially of the theatre. They follow a certain form, adumbrate a set of rules, require the participation of an audience. Greek tragedy required the death of the Hero. Medieval tragedy celebrated the death of the Saviour. Renaissance tragedy brought back the Hero, not as myth, but as one of us.

Tragedy enacted is staged. Staging requires artifice. It must follow a narrative protocol. It stipulates a rhetorical skill, like the skills of a playwright, which Will Shakespeare had in abundance, and Elizabethan tragedy is still effective for us. George Steiner has claimed that we have already witnessed *The Death of Tragedy*, because poetic language no longer holds the central position it once did in the times of Dante and Shakespeare. But tragedy can be staged today, on the stage, in new and different ways. The random falls of earth around the grave-like setting of Pina Bausch's *Viktor* are banal and repetitive events that in context take on a deeper meaning, and open the door to the tragic sense. Tragedy, like comedy, touches on the absurd. In comedy the inadmissible is released in laughter, in tragedy it is released in catharsis, the return to the absurdity of life that is accompanied by a renewal of compassion.

The tragic abounds in all traditional art that starts from grandeur. It deals with figures staged so as to create a narrative, for which the title is often an essential script. The heroic event was the culminating theme of all serious painting, and is still clearly alive with Poussin and not too distant in Claude. But in both we sense a diminution of belief, a surge of the merely aesthetic. Can the tragic survive this loss of belief?

If architecture, whose tropes are unspoken, cannot so clearly evoke a heroic past, it has still been associated with the heroic scale of values. Architecture provided the framework for the epic sculptures placed in the pediments of the Greek temples. It was admitted not for itself but for the setting it provided by which the sacred could be made accessible and approached by ordinary people. We can argue that this role at least is still open to it today.

Landscape with Psyche and the Palace of Love
Claude, 1664

Landscape with Psyche and the Palace of Love,
detail of the pictured building
Claude

With Claude, architecture acquires an expressive presence linking it to the heroic event enacted in the foreground. There is a Claude in the National Gallery titled *Landscape with Psyche and the Palace of Love*, and we all know that the palace is a building type. So architecture has been willingly incorporated into the fable. And as in the representation, so in the construction of the social world, it became an essential channel for myth to enter daily life. During the Baroque, it was expected to confer gravitas, where needed, and it is easy to recognise it in Borromini, here in San Carlino alle Quattro Fontane, where the cornice joins the four apses of the plan and their separating straight pieces in one fell swoop, without pause, without the brakes that re-entrants above the columns would have applied. The speed of this cornice is unexpected and disturbing: it brings an aspect of the sublime into play. It questions the convention, it rejects the ordinary.

San Carlino alle Quattro Fontane
Borromini, 1667

Christ Church, Spitalfields
Nicholas Hawksmoor, 1729

In such examples we cannot claim that the tragic is directly expressed in architecture, but that in mediating the worship of the Hero-Redeemer the activity for which the church is intended, it partakes of the tragic. Without it, the mystery of faith could not enter ordinary life.

After the *terribilità* evoked in Mannerism, the Baroque is more closely linked to matters of faith, the whole trauma of the counter-reformation. Yet one senses very little about faith in the somewhat political programme of building city churches during the time of Wren and Hawksmoor, and the return of a subdued sense of the terrible in Hawksmoor seems to have more to do with the autonomy of architecture, with freely rearranging its syntax, evolved for a sacred purpose, no doubt, but now concerned with exploring more abstract possibilities. In the eighteenth century the element of myth, still alive in the Baroque, finally disappeared, and presaged the coming of modernity at the end of the nineteenth century.

With Piranesi, one can make more of a case that the original drawings do indeed express a feeling in their own right, a feeling close to a sense of the destiny of man and of his frailty. For Piranesi the building was an essential means by which to approach high emotions. He had an eye for ruins, and the ancient world lay all about him in ruins. To depict the fall of architecture came close to depicting the fall of man. And even when he

Tomb of the Metelli, (from *Antichi Romane*)
Piranesi

Temple of Vesta, (from *Prima Parte*)
Piranesi

constructed a fictive world, as with his fantasy on the Temple of Vesta, we sense the limits of attainment, the arbitrariness of design, the hubris of man, who now appears dwarfed by his own creations. Even more does Boullée shrink man to tiny dimensions, so that in a world of heroic stature, he is of no more significance than an ant. Boullée's Stadium, with its escape stairs shown in abstract section, is like an anticipation of the Pompidou Centre, it reduces man to being part of a crowd. All grandeur has been absorbed by the building.

Stadium: facade and section
Etienne-Louis Boullée

Centre Pompidou, Paris, escalator
Piano and Rogers, 1976

The decline of heroic status was already implied in the eighteenth century search for the sublime, where man is confronted by the limits beyond which nature is indifferent to his destiny. On the one hand, the heroic becomes visible as a fiction; on the other, nature becomes visible as a machine. The machine aesthetic, insofar as it denies humanity and prefers a studied indifference, raises a certain pathos, if it does not quite touch the sublime. With the Romantics, this indifference has undermined belief and generated a new sense that man is alone.

La Liberté Guidant le Peuple
Delacroix, 1830

La Liberté Guidant le Peuple, detail of background
Delacroix

Delacroix's *Liberty Leading the People* is a figure of rhetoric, an abstraction made vivid by the use of the female form. Man is free, but he has no witness; unless it is architecture that now provides that witness, reflecting as it does the weight of society, marking the action with its indisputable evidence of Time and Place. Social justice replaces theological retribution.

Enigma of the Day
De Chirico, 1914

Chief
Franz Kline, 1950

And as the metaphysical limits of art itself become visible, around World War One, art returns to the theme of the building as witness, now reinforced by its capacity to represent not only social reality, but through its recurrence in dreams, becoming even a kind of surrogate conscience, or embodiment of memory. But this demands that art exercises a capacity of representation. Both abstraction and conceptual thought, the over-riding discoveries of twentieth century art, cast a doubt over representation, substituting the art object as itself the final mystery of life. Abstract art transfers attention from object-as-means to object-as-end. The art object no longer offers itself as a window on to life, but directly engages our cognitive faculties. By becoming an enigma, it resists being emptied of meaning. Instead of meaning, we have meaningfulness.

With Franz Kline, with Robert Motherwell, we accede to the power of the gesture, but we still obstinately attempt to animate the figure. We search the gesture for a meaning. We take the title as clue, as script. And indeed, each form embodies a strong character that stirs ambiguous associations and stimulates the imagination. The very name of Abstract Expressionism suggests that something is expressed, that some content has survived.

I was much struck by Sean Scully's recent review of a Rothko retrospective. (*TLS*, 6 November 1998). Scully, who is an artist as well as a critic, denies that abstraction supplants all figurative content, insists that Rothko's severe rectangles still constitute figures. As figures, they are receptive to the projections we can bring to them, and they are nothing if not emotive. Richard Cork has said: "We cannot help seeing in these great veils of orange, red, black, yellow or maroon a host of possible references to the visible world."

Rothko seems to be a special case, even for devotees of pure aesthetics. He is among those abstractionists, including Agnes Martin, whose very restricted system insinuates a moral stance. His early paintings were more figurative, and the ever-increasing austerity throughout his life suggests renunciation. The word tragic has been applied to his work, without referring particularly to the coincidence of the final black works and his subsequent suicide.

Francis Bacon, in his conversations with David Sylvester, spoke of a method of portraiture that seeks to isolate the subject as a sort of event staged within a frame. The background is clean, elegant, complete; in context, the smeared paint on the face, the distortion of the figure, take on a suggestion of movement, of something glimpsed rather than seen. This is analogous to the method by which Heidegger deals with essence, no longer something that can be fully grasped, but something that still leaves a kind of cultural trace. By metaphoric extension this sense of a fugitive presence, through Bacon's magic, succeeds in communicating an impression of life and pain. What he wanted to do, he said, was to isolate the image and take it away from the interior and the home.

In espousing this ambition Bacon sets up a dialectic in which the interior and the home are seen as private and makeshift, and a public realm emerges which is identified with something inescapable, like a judgment and a destiny. He evidently wants to reinstate a sense of the human condition defined by loss and pain. His use of triptychs in a secular situation signals that the mystery has stepped down from the altar and invaded private

Lights Red over Black
Rothko, 1957

Portrait of George Dyer in a Mirror, 1968
Francis Bacon, 1968

life. This is surely close to a tragic view of life. It is of course an interesting paradox that many of the settings depict the interior and the home in lurid terms, showing the horror encountered in bedrooms and bathrooms, and the desperation that assails the individual at his most naked and vulnerable.

Bacon uses a combination of abstraction and figuration, and let us acknowledge that there is nothing in art theory to deny this method. The difference between the two modes acts as a framing device, suggesting two different levels of existence. In the staging of meaning, particular advantage may be taken of a combination of both. Where realism tends to kill the life it depicts (as with Soviet Realism) a measure of abstraction, by stepping back from life, may suggest life more vividly.

Malevich's famous image of Suprematist Architecture montaged on to a photograph of New York suggests the displacement of the old by the new, in an opposition where the new is accorded the advantage of artistic expression, so that it can speak for the future. In Cassandre's poster for Nord Express the abstracted handling of the locomotive's mechanism, privileged as art, also suggests actual movement more vividly that a photograph would have done. In both cases, the change of style acts as a framing device to intensify the meaning.

Within architecture, in the course of the twentieth century, abstract forms have triumphed at the expense of symbolic resonance. With the loss of the classical orders, there is no upstanding metaphor for the human figure, a fact that gives peculiar interest to John Outram's invention of the "robot order" made from service ducts. With the literal interpretation of functionality, architecture is reduced to a utility, deprived of expression, expected to reveal nothing but the physical trace of human movement. The

Photo-montage with *Suprematist Architecture*
Malevich, 1923

Poster for *Nord Express*
Cassandre, 1927

"machine for living" places a particular stress on the ergonomic aspects that literally fit the body, such as the mechanisms of bathroom and kitchen, staircase and ramp.

The machine for living took exemplary form with the Villa Savoye; in museums the same approach can result in a complete complex of ramps, escalators, elevators and staircases, conduits and outlets comprising a total life-support system, more appropriate to the conquest of space than to the exploration of culture. The Archigram idea assumed that the resources available for the military exploration of space should be appropriated to the enjoyment of ordinary citizens. The service system, as art object, here assumes transcendental importance, and nothing is left of the privilege Aristotle assigned to architecture, to at least provide the site where fine art may celebrate the sacred myths.

In its most extreme as a mere servant, in the form of the shopping mall, architecture has no voice of its own. Management of the mall includes management of its architecture. But oddly, life attains its own momentum, no matter into what receptacle it is poured. The High-Tech atrium has now been so widely imitated that it means no more now than that the developer wants to be in the swim. The atrium pioneered at the Eaton Centre in Toronto has become a commonplace of shopping malls, indeed of public buildings. As a functional device, its aim is not to uplift the spirit but to provide the pleasurable sensations that encourage retail sales. If this precludes the tragic, as it must surely do, this is hardly surprising. If the overwhelming totality of functional architecture is dedicated to an everyday banality, it can hardly be expected to rise to a higher plane of expression. Yet today, after Gehry's Guggenheim, at Bilbao, anything can be any shape. Gehry has restored expression to a central place.

To seek the tragic in modern architecture, we may have to follow Adolf Loos' injunction to return to the tomb and the monument, where physical functionality as such has no weight. In Scarpa's Tomb and Cemetery for the Brion-Vega family at San Vito, however, it is not the purpose of the building that affects us so much as the extreme concentration on detail. If anyone was to convince us that "God is in the detail" it is Scarpa. It is difficult to explain this effect. We are somehow dislocated from our ordinary view of things: but we are not returned to the object-in-itself, but to a sense of the importance of seeing, an opening of the inner eye. Stirling is very different, he is brusque where Scarpa is precious, but there is an extraordinary moment at the Staatsgalerie where the main gallery, with its coved cornice, draws back to admit the bulge of the central drum, creating an enormous compression of space that, again, refreshes our sense of being alive. Both Scarpa and Stirling are architects who question the ordinary and expose us to the unexpected, and renew our sense of the human condition.

Church of the Light, Ibaraki, Osaka
Tadao Ando, 1989

O House
Tadao Ando, 1988

With Ando's Church of the Light we have a strange reversal of values. The Christian cross was always seen in the West as solid, the indubitable Thing on which the God-Hero was killed. Ando, from outside the Christian fold, is able to see it as space, so undeniably renewing our sense of its symbolic meaning. This drawing back from the oppression of Western muscularity can also produce a Zenian sense of the fullness of space, through underlining the potency of emptiness, as we see here in his O House of 1998. These are examples of an architecture which is not directed squarely at the idea of mechanism, but that still works through the physical to engender a sense of values that I would roughly describe as spiritual. Does this approach the tragic? No, but it allows the possibility of the tragic to come close. Architecture can be expressive, and the tragic is not precluded by any principle that I know.

Certain architects have seen themselves as tragic figures, and Charles Jencks has shown how that category applies to Le Corbusier. He read Nietzsche, he saw himself as a protagonist of great art, engaged in a struggle to balance the intellectual and the lyrical, in order to realise the potential of the epoch. Something of this struggle adheres to many of his works: if they are not the staging of a tragedy they undeniably have a tragic force. The buildings at Chandigarh, like Lou Kahn's buildings at Dacca, address human life in heroic terms, and raise an awareness of the power of hubris, the fatal flaw that brings the Hero down. But my choice of the tragic in architecture comes to rest on the image of Aldo Rossi's Gallaratese housing in Milan. It is itself a comment on Chandigarh, I have no doubt, and just as Corbu mixes the machine with the grandiloquent, so does Rossi.

Housing at Gallaratese, Milan
Aldo Rossi, 1973

Housing at Gallaratese: detail of the fat columns
Aldo Rossi

The fat columns are not rational, they deliberately cancel out the rational premise of the entire design. The break in the regularity creates a framing device, proclaiming an ironic self-awareness. It thereby induces a matching awareness in us, placing us in the role of audience confronting something deliberately staged. Rossi made many drawings of this motif, clearly it was intentionally a figure, in the sense that Scully applies to Rothko. In its combination of the lyrical and the intellectual, it speaks for the impossibility of achieving perfection. In that sense, and for those who can read the book of architecture, it makes a truly tragic statement. But this value is only apparent when the built work is interpreted in context.

If we consider how important context is for the staging of opera, we can begin to see how architecture, once built, takes on as setting a fullness that it does not have within its own autonomy. Bernard Tschumi appreciated this in his *Manhattan Transcripts*. In opera we observe how music, libretto, lighting, choreography, staging, casting even, all independent areas of decision, all separate systems, are separately nebulous; but, coordinated, can achieve dramatic effect and move the spirit in powerful ways. At the moment when a busy stage empties, lights reduce to a single spot focused centre stage on a man and woman, and the orchestra goes from full spate to solo oboe, we have no difficulty in construing the meaning. Architecture as the setting of social space, in its wide reach from the quotidian to the moment of personal epiphany, is capable of responding to emotion, and of placing the entirely personal into the entirely social.

London, February 1999; lecture given 16 March, published in Architectural Design, October 2000.

Walter Bor takes us to RM's Southwood Lawn Road flats to visit his friend Katherine Thompson for tea, 28 March.

RM asks her: "What do you find wrong about these flats?" Answer: "The kitchen is a little cramped."

Norwich trip: we visit Barney and Sophie, and have lunch with Terry Farrell at Upland House, 2/5 April.

Lecture: *Modernism and Aftermath—a personal view of the 70s*, Twentieth Century Society Conference, 9 April.

Peter Carolin asks for a piece about the Smithsons for *ARQ*.

CRITIQUE OF THE SMITHSONS *WITHOUT RHETORIC*
INSIGHT PIECE IN *ARCHITECTURAL RESEARCH QUARTERLY*
Helena Webster, Academy Editions, 1997

When I went to teach at the Bartlett, my interest was to investigate meaning in architecture, the title of a book soon to be written by Jencks and Baird. Before long I was giving a course called "Meaning in Architecture", without measuring anything, but using lots of comparisons (twin slide projectors had become all the rage). The motivation had been provided by reading English translations of Ferdinand de Saussure's *Course in General Linguistics*, which came out in 1966, and Roland Barthes' *Elements of Semiology*.[1] Thus provided with a radical interpretation of how meaning in language worked through association, it was great fun to try to extend this methodology from verbal to non-verbal systems of expression, as indeed Barthes himself set out to do.[2]

The confluence of ideas seemed to be confirmed when one of my heroes, Angela Carter, published an article in *New Society* titled "Notes for a Theory of Sixties Style" which dealt with the meaning of the dress sported by the beat generation.[3] She followed this up by another article titled "Fin de Siècle".[4] The first was optimistic, the second pessimistic, in terms of her enthusiasm for freedom of expression. Mary Douglas, then a colleague at University College, was another who dealt with contemporary culture, pointing to the biblical element in the long hair sported by rock singers. The interest for me lay in the fact that for meaning to be established, a certain convention had to rule, the breaking of which was visible as the radical note. And why not extend this principle to architecture? In a way, dress was the easiest step, since everybody dressed, and one could argue about blue jeans, worn by almost everyone in the room—were they an act of defiance or an act of conformity? If they were radical once, when had they become conventional? The progress of the radical into the conventional became a fascinating aspect of the transformations going on, enabling one to point to change as change of meaning.

In the course of learning about semiology, I learned to distinguish between poetry and rhetoric. Poetry was meant to be fresh, to break moulds, to create new meanings. Rhetoric was meant to persuade, and to do this it had to be made up of things and attitudes that everyone could understand. Poetry, like Greek civilisation, was good, it signified renewal; rhetoric, like the Romans, was bad, it signified more of the same. One spoke of 'mere rhetoric', meaning a stopgap offered in place of real action. At the same time, rhetoric was in some sense unavoidable. Because it drew on common factors that individuals could recognise, it embodied the shared assumptions that make up a society. It was the main means of communication. But this division made a problem: art could only be radical, be new, unfamiliar: how then could it communicate with ordinary people? Architecture was in a worse state, because it was charged with the duty of being right for ordinary people.

Then here comes this book from the pens of the Smithsons, *Without Rhetoric, an Architectural Aesthetic*, claiming that it was possible to build without rhetoric, to build in some way according to a deeper truth, giving a new lift to the idea of functional understanding, a fresh claim for the redemption implicit in the very idea of modern architecture.[5] Functionalism had allied itself with science, wishing to look beneath the conventional surface to find a reality more powerful than appearance, wishing to break with convention, and invent a new future. An architecture without rhetoric is evidently an architecture that does not set out to persuade, yet somehow convinces. How is this to come about? It seems to imply an architecture in all respects justified by its conditions of use, free from pomp and ceremony, perhaps therefore an architecture of essentials. As a title, it seems to be didactic in intent, seeking to justify a poetic strangeness by creating a sense of inevitability.

Compare the Smithsons' *House of the Future* and their pavilion in the This is Tomorrow exhibition: between them lies a dialectical space. Both projects break with convention; but one employs the promise of technology to look forward to the future, while the other looks back to the archetype of the truly human, reminding us of fundamentals. There is thus a concern to enter the future without shedding humanity. The truly human has already given evidence of existing, and is not still to be discovered only through the pressure of empirical events. When they came to design a small house in a Watford suburb for Derek Sugden, it was not so much a house of the future, as a house for all time. It contains the very archetype of the rural house, one that is strangely familiar.

As a teacher at the AA Peter coined an aphorism: "Mies is great, but Corb communicates." Mies and Corb were two principle sources of the Smithson aesthetic, and in the difference between them it is possible to see the same dialectical opposition, one standing for reason and control, the other for excitement and provocation. It is possible then to view their work as stretched between opposing concepts of (to use their own phrase) "continuity and newness".[6]

When they came to design their Economist Building, there was a return to order. The models that were uppermost were from Mies.[7] There is a regular rhythm in the arrangement of the mullions, providing a calm visual surface and the look of stone, which binds the structural grid into the ground and into the city. The small piazza is a decent space, not a wind-blown desert. There is not only a lesson in urban building, but a lesson in urban structuring. They evoke the Virgilian dream in Corb's vision of bringing space to the city:

> *This is what draws us to his Capitol group at Chandigarh; its patrician sense of space, its calm, its control… this is why we return so often to*

Lafayette Park… to feel again its decent calm, its openness, to study its methods of putting the car in its place, all achieved without rhetoric…. This is why the Chase Manhattan Bank fascinates—its technology and its mechanisms are under control—it has no rhetoric.[8]

Rhetoric here is equated with undue emphasis, with the blatant thrusting forward of technological expression as no longer a means but an end. The end should be pleasure, the enjoyment of life. Mere mechanisms should not intrude on this humanistic goal. Smithson cites the absence of fuss with inventions that have already been absorbed into life, like going up in a modern lift: the doors close, there is silence, the doors open. The machinery functions as part of the background.[9]

The calm surface stands for the role of architecture as inducement to a settled life, as a setting for life, rather than the substitute for it. To designate this anonymity as a peculiarly honest sort of aesthetic, however, betrays the desire for life and art to merge into one. Along with the mechanisms, artistic intentions also retreat into the background, true; but as background they take on the aura of necessity. The good result is thought of as coming about naturally, without resort to artifice. The result is achieved "without rhetoric".

However, they do not deny that they are constructing an architectural aesthetic, and an aesthetic offered as exemplar is a means of persuasion. It is no less dependent on the use of rhetoric as is an aesthetic of exposed pipes and services; like the priest in Barthes' *Mythologies*, whose hair was always slightly mussed, but always in the same way, so carefully careless, the absence of insistence becomes itself the sign for honesty. It is similar to the rhetoric of plain speaking. The Economist Building is a highly successful example of business architecture taking on a responsible public face. Between the simple structure and the stone grid of appearance lies a great deal of design effort, which the architects felt the need to dissimulate.

Useless to argue with Peter about that, and I tried; he wasn't interested in the theory of signs as such, although he believed that a building intended for public use should all the time signal how it was intended to be used. The interest was kept to a purely architectonic level. The Doric order, for example, was exemplary in signifying how it was put together from primary architectonic elements. As far as Peter was concerned, the Doric went soft around 450 BC, long before it reached the masterful artifice of the Parthenon.[10] In wider culture, it became only a metaphor. But this insistence on limiting their interpretations to what was architectonically important did not hinder the Smithsons from returning again and again to the ancient sites, gratifying their sheer enjoyment of great architecture however it came about.

Their view of place is sensitive to all the nuances that give a great place its uniqueness, and its richness as a cultural achievement. Peter's book *Bath: Walks within the Walls*, gives ample proof of this respect for place and history, as well as showing the capacity of being able to get you to look closely at the object of study, that made him such a great teacher. He talks about the essence of a place.[11] He takes in the texture of the city as a whole, but also the simplicity and grandeur of Wood's Royal Crescent.

It was an appreciation of how well old towns work that caused the Smithsons to be less than damning about several pieces of make-believe that could be seen as, to some extent, reflecting popular taste and enjoyment. One place that interested them, but failed to satisfy, was Port Grimaud. It undoubtedly succeeded in its aim to communicate with ordinary people, but only at the expense of creating a fiction, a unit of consumption for a privileged few, not a serious advance in closing the gap between the radical and the popular. For the gap between the strangely new and the familiar old was potentially the space of alienation, and the dialectical process by which they related made a problem for the architect who wished to communicate. The new in its raw state was not part of communication, it first had to be formalised, made into an idea.

One dramatic sentence of *Without Rhetoric* reads: "Things become ideas only very slowly."[12] This is true. Consider the time that it took Corb to develop the idea of a modern factory that he glimpsed in the canonic factory he illustrates in *Vers une architecture* into his own design for a factory built at Saint-Dié in 1951. Consider the time it took from the building of Berlage's Holland House in London in 1914, with its all over mullion wall in glazed ceramic, to the development of a full aesthetic of steel and glass, as in Mies' Lake Shore Drive of 1951. It takes that sort of time for things that are under your eyes to become disposable within culture.

The Smithsons remained modern architects, but they accepted the limitations of architecture. It can no longer be seen as a quick fix for society, because culture is a deeper and more complex entity than the theory of function can handle. If it takes time for an idea to form, then architecture as a radical art form is strangely inhibited. Their recent buildings have been modest in scope, and strangely penitential in feeling. I suspect that their feeling for people has somehow got the better of them. If we expected a lot more, and if we are disappointed, I think we must acknowledge the inhibitions that prevented them from simply becoming successful members of the establishment. An enormous honesty, that would not tolerate half-solutions, and an integrity that left them always questing for a real point of entry to the labyrinth of the human psyche.

London, October 1998, published 31 March 1999.

1. Which I had acquired in 1963.

2. With his *Système de la mode*.

3. In *New Society,* 14 December 1967.

4. In *New Society*, 17 August 1972.

5. *Without Rhetoric*—an *Architectural Aesthetic* 1955–1972, London, Latimer New Dimensions, 1973.

6. From *Without Rhetoric*, p. 88.

7. They refer not only to the Mies of Lafayette Park, 1959, but to the evolved Mies of SOM in the Chase Manhattan Bank, 1961.

8. From *Without Rhetoric*, pp. 14–16.

9. From *Without Rhetoric*, p. 48.

10. From *Without Rhetoric*, pp. 52–53.

11. From *Without Rhetoric*, p. 81. Criticising modern development insensitive to context; the text continues: *at a deeper level we felt that these acts were an insult to the essence of those villages and cities. We have since come to realise what a huge personal mental convulsion is needed to allow us even to think about this essence. It seemed to demand a sensibility that present-day architects do not have trained into them.*

12. From *Without Rhetoric*, p. 56. On the time needed for ideas to form: *It has always taken a very long time for a useful thing to become an idea—to acquire formal value… to have a place amongst other ideas… to become capable of being defined, adjusted, perfected, rejected, re-perfected in the mind—often almost to the point of losing the practical intention of the original thing.*

Colin Rowe has heart attack/stroke, May.

RIBA awards Royal Gold Medal to City of Barcelona: RM writes and pronounces citation, 3 June.

Hasegawa gives Annual Discourse at the Royal Academy, 25 June.

Celia begins construction of her Garden Studio: slab on piles, brick, cedar, steel, tern-coated roof, 30 June.

Celia goes to France solo, to take part in the *réunion annuelle*, she uses the Paddington express, 21/24 August.

RM attends a Mary Douglas event, her goodbye, in the Haldane Room at UCL, 23 September.

He realises that for all her gentleness, she is a strong person and speaks with authority.

Reception at National Portrait Gallery, Ed's triumph; B & C supper at Café Delancey, 19 October.

To dinner with Ricky Burdett for Wilf Wang: Zaha, Mohsen and Home, etc, 22 October.

Lampugnani lectures at the AA, RM at dinner afterwards, notes how he turns his head to each speaker in turn, just as if he were following the tennis at Wimbledon, 2 November.

Colin Rowe dies after suffering a stroke some months earlier, 5 November.

RM lectures at Greenwich on *The Critical Act* (Stirling and Bacon) for Ivana Wingham, 5 November.

RM goes to Cambridge for Taina Rikala's PhD defence: all OK; meets Tim Benton, 15 November.

Rogers book launch at 88 Wood Street; we give dinner to the Brawnes at Coq d'Argent, 17 November.

B to Hugh Casson memorial service at St Paul's cathedral, chats with Neville Conder, 29 November.

RM lectures at UCE Birmingham on *The Critical Act* for Taina Rikala, 30 November.

Alan Powers' book launch at the Art Workers' Guild, 3 December.

Celia sees two young foxes playing in the back garden.

Lunch with Melinda and David, and Harrison Birtwistle, 31 December.

RM plays keyboard, with Mike Gold on sax, for John and Su's millennium party; we march to Primrose Hill behind piper to view fireworks on the river, 31 December.

A photo of Bob and Mike playing is on display in the bedroom corridor at Villa Jones, Bargemon.

2000

Completion of Celia's Garden Studio. Next, restoration of garden with new lawn and bird bath, January.

To USA for Rowe events: Washington, Cosmos Club; New York, Princeton Club, 4 to 10 February.

RM speaks first of 18 in Rowe Memorial in Carnegie Institution organised by Judy di Maio.

Judy makes a great speech: she says when she hears thunder she thinks it's Colin up there moving the furniture.

ROWE IN MEMORIAM

When I entered the Liverpool School of Architecture I came to Colin's attention through my sketch designs, which happened every other Tuesday. On these occasions a band of sophisticated sophomores came around to check out the freshmen, and I was picked out for my brevity and wit. What for me was tryout, done out of pure naivety, for Colin was evidence of independent thinking. Subsequently, he was apt to attribute to me intentions far beyond my means. Colin used flattery, not for his own advantage, but to improve his circle of friends. He soon converted me to Corb, but later preferred to think it was I who did that to him, since, he said, it gave him a lot of grief.

Colin spoke always with a touch of irony, with complete knowingness. His awareness was total, yet his feelings were real, never affected. The insistence on seeing architecture as a unique intersection of thought and feeling gave his criticism an indubitably personal note. His words were persuasive, because he always addressed you directly, privately. This quality, translated to his written texts, allowed him to make insinuations that were compulsive, without ever asserting conclusions that went beyond the evidence. No wonder that he influenced so dramatically the teaching of architecture in the States, by linking studio to history and theory.

Colin visited us once in London at a time when I was struggling with three children on an inadequate income. Looking round my improvised living room he protested: "Robert, how can you live in such squalor?" "But Colin, it's just temporary." "My dear Robert, I was under the impression that LIFE was temporary."

London, February 2000, given Washington, 16 February 2000.

News of the death of Wayland; we go to France for his funeral: Hotel Sévigné, Grignan.

RM publishes *Education for the Creative Act* in ARQ, Cambridge University, vol. 4 no. 1.

Technology bubble bursts; share prices begin to drop, March.

To Marlborough for Melinda and David's wedding, service of blessing in Alton Barnes church, 10 June.

We attend Terry Farrell's Inaugural as Professor of Architecture at University of Westminster, 14 June.

To Royal Academy for lecture by Danny Libeskind, and dinner, 17 June.

Mary Wall's goodbye at the AA: she is off to work in the States, 23 June.

To Chichester for opening of Sandy's gallery at Pallant, 24 June.

RM is reading all the novels of Patrick Modiano.

RA Forum on *Return of the Subject* follow-up, and dinner, 7 July.

We go to Paolozzi show at Flowers East; then on to Stephen's for tea, 8 July.

RM in juries at LSE, then at reception in Ziggurat Building, chez Richard Sennett, 28 July.

To Brentwood to collect a timber plinth for Jim Stirling's bust, 1 August.

Weekend with Sally Shearman, stay at Papplewick Hall; visit Villa Caldogno replica, 12/13 August.

It really is a replica of the Villa Caldogno, carried out with archeological precision.

Done by a bloke called Hugh Matheson, of the Hong Kong family: he showed us round.

Although one of the smallest, it has a grand scale, and looks magnificent in South Nottinghamshire.

We go to Cambridge for C's site meeting, then to Eleanor where we give supper to Carrie Cocke and Nick Ray, having visited his work at Clare Hall, 8 August.

A VISIT TO CLARE HALL
FOR *ARCHITECTURE TODAY*

Clare Hall, like Darwin, is dedicated to research: its inhabitants include mature scholars with established reputations as fellows or visitors, and younger scholars with wives or husbands, and often children, whose careers are still under design. The mix is more varied than in an undergraduate college, and this shows in a certain maturity, not only of the individual students encountered on a Monday morning, but in the atmosphere, relaxed and not at all institutional, of the interior spaces. And that in turn seemed to derive at least in part from the informal interiors bequeathed by Ralph Erskine, who, as a member of Team 10, was devoted to the creation of social space. Like the Smithsons, he looked for 'patterns of association' that could bring effectiveness to the architectural idea. These interiors are still both liveable and loved.

So this is a case of a valued environment, and a wished-for continuity. Nick Ray worked with Erskine on the Michael Stoker Building, next to the original building of 1969, and completed eighteen years later, in 1987. There are some differences, but the two buildings use the same language and together set the tone for the first courtyard, completed with the construction of the Brian Pippard Building by Nicholas Ray Associates in 1997. This too continues to use some of the same language, notably the one-way monopitch rising along the length, and a near-matching brick (the original being no longer obtainable).

However, some details now begin to show a different spirit. The cantilevered reinforced concrete beams projecting from the brickwork are now proscribed by building regulations as the source of cold bridging; instead, panels of silver grey ceramic tiles are used to tie together the ranges of windows, and steel lintols and balconies to provide surface interest. The use of metal perhaps betrays a wish to be up-to-date, while the detailing of the internal handrail with closely spaced supports takes on a distinctly arty-crafty look: it is hardly surprising to find that the designer (Ken Caldwell, the director in charge) is from Ayrshire and studied at the Mackintosh School of Art.

With the Anthony Low Building, we have something different: it is a brick-walled cubic block, geometrically precise, but deeply indented on the north side facing the garden, where the extent of the cut-out isolates the corner pillar. That in itself reminds one of Rob Krier's Dickes House of 1974, except that the pillar is not rounded and white, but in brick that maintains the planes of the walls, and maintains also the air of functional decorum, cooperating with the exposed steel detailing of floor beams and balustrades. The deep indentation accommodates the swoop of the brick path, but also allows sunlight to strike from behind on the inner face of the north-facing balcony.

With yellow paint used on the reveals of the top-light above the staircase to warm even the diffused northern sky, and with the bar placed at the back of the space like a hearth, we have a cheerful interior that faces north to the quadrangle and yet stays sunny a lot of the time. The building, completed in June 2000, was in response to a request from the graduate students to have their own common room. The bursar, checking for debris or breakages after a weekend of partying, was mildly surprised and slightly disturbed to find everything shipshape and in order. Although it is a pavilion-in-the-garden, it looks resolutely towards that space as a hallowed quadrangle, the outer side of which, closing out Grange Road, is formed by Elmside, a house by Edward Prior, together with the renovated library and a group of study rooms. The result is a building that encourages its role as club, and so takes its social use as a given, in the Erskine tradition, without aping Erskine's style. It is more geometrically precise and contained; although one might feel—as I did—that the size of the cutout in balcony and entrance overhang almost swamps the residual body of the cube.

The latest addition to the college is a residential group forming a new courtyard (West Court) that perforce takes its cue from the adjoining group of buildings in white-painted brickwork. This group of houses was built in the 1960s by Lord Rothschild in a somewhat unusual style which makes an effect more *fin-de-siècle* than heroic modern. The college bought the Rothschild house quite recently, and Nicholas Ray Associates made flats for Visiting Fellows in it. The new buildings, named after Robert Honeycombe and Paul Mellon, together provide 11 more flats and 13 graduate rooms, with associated common rooms, so that the addition is considerably larger than the existing house. Even with a general recognition of the college's need to expand, that made a delicate issue for the planners within their West Cambridge guidelines. They took some time over it, and insisted on some changes that have the effect of breaking down the simple masses and breaking up the elevations. This was a favourite response of planners when I started practicing in 1951. Although commissioned in mid-1997, the project was not completed until May 2000.

This resistance explains the delicate balance sought between white painted brickwork and grey metal sheathing. Ken Caldwell has made a studied combination of metal on the courtyard side and slates on the outside. This has produced a very clever play with scale: the graduate rooms seen from the courtyard look like two-storied houses, helped by the landscape being raised along their frontage. The access to the upper level study bedrooms comes via the double-height gallery in the south wing, and this terminates at top level in rather impressive lookout windows at the gable ends, providing plenty of incident for the planners and some real sense of presence. The overall character is not too far from Baillie Scott, yet also looks strictly contemporary. Add some judicious colours for the stucco at the entrance points, and you have a sweet blend of the domestic and the institutional.

Working within the Erskine legacy, Nicholas Ray Associates have thus earned their spurs as college architects in the high tradition of socially responsive architecture. College buildings must always be sensitive to their surroundings, but in this case the sensitivity is not overdone, and the result is both acceptable and lively.

London, October 2000, published October 2000.

On vacation in Greece: fly to Kalamata; rent a red Nissan; stay chez Lela; swimming at Stoupa, 10/24 September.

RM likes that, because it's sandy; and a spring on the right cools the water without making it cold.

The fishing port at Stoupa was visited 20 years ago, view of harbour unchanged: see watercolour.

Lecture given at the Royal Academy (*Can the Tragic Appear in Architecture?*) is published in *Architectural Design* for October 2000, edited by Richard Patterson.

We throw Silver Wedding party at Mall Studios for 30 guests: "Silver Sunday", a great success, 8 October.

Jeremy Dixon comes for a drink and to check the text of the piece he has asked B to write for *Architecture Today*.

BOOK ON DIXON JONES
TEXT FOR BOOK ON *DIXON JONES*

No project associated with Jeremy Dixon and Edward Jones ever had such visibility as the design for Northampton City Hall, the glass pyramid; and the design for the Royal Opera House is so set about by circumstance that it hardly restores that visibility. Both they, and architecture, have changed since that competition win of 1972. Since then they have worked apart, now again together. The conditions of practice are now more demanding. As their joint practice gains in cohesion, it also must accommodate an unprecedented complexity not only of the building, both in its internal organisation and in its interface with the city, but of the cultural conditions within which the building is to be judged. That is why there is a special interest to be found in their designs for the Royal Opera House and the National Portrait Gallery. In both cases the commissions were the result of a competition, and so are based not only on circumstance, but on a set of ideas. Yet in both cases the site is so embedded in previous acts of building and in the congestion of the city that the new architecture must look carefully around before taking the least step into space.

An Opera House is a machine for spectacle. The longitudinal section of Charles Garnier's Opera House, lavishly depicted in Bannister Fletcher, never failed to astonish one as a student. In spite of the grandeur of the auditorium with its staircase and foyer and the celebration of occasion that it implies, the importance of the social spaces is exceeded by the sheer size of the staging arrangements and fly tower. And the fly tower, of which an impressive view can be had from the nearby roof garden of Galeries Lafayette, was not left out of the story, it was as richly accoutred with the necessary ordonnance and symbols of Neoclassical architecture as was the main entrance front.

So what it comprised was two vast interlocking systems in delicate equilibrium: theatre as enjoyment and theatre as effort—the mechanism of social display and the mechanism of thespian representation—both necessary, both acknowledged and voiced in the architecture. Artifice was inseparable from staging, but it was espoused in the name of truth. With the external volumes so completely echoing the disposition of necessary spaces, the dome of the auditorium virtually crashing into the fly tower, the whole thing was an example of functionalism *avant la lettre*. But was it not also an illustration of the kind of Beaux Arts elaboration that the arch-functionalist Le Corbusier was trying to persuade us to cast out as effete? Confined as I was by Corbusian rationalism, it was some time before it finally dawned that nothing could be more rational, or more persuasive. In this building, Garnier, proficient in the social ideals of his time, created a masterpiece which is as dedicated to decorum as it is to performance. Big it is, but in proportion, and all on axis, since it occupies an isolated site.

The Royal Opera House of Covent Garden has an altogether more complicated history. On a site first occupied by a theatre in 1732, it took its present form with EM Barry's design of 1858 (beating Paris by three years, we note) but since greatly altered. By now it is locked into the city fabric, and while the grip of the city is tighter, the demands of the programme are tougher. The fly tower was expanded in 1902 and is now greatly enlarged. Rehearsals have become always more demanding as the schedule of performances becomes more complex, and staging itself is always increasing in complexity, so there are many more rehearsal spaces to be accommodated, and the space needed for scenery is far more than just the fly tower. There was a moment in 1974 when the Floral Hall was taken over for scenery storage, but this was an interim measure. By today, the demands of the staging system for international opera have grown beyond what was necessary in 1902, and far beyond what might have been contemplated in 1861, when Garnier won his competition. An enormous additional area must now be found for the storage, preparation and manipulation of sets, in all about six times more than the area of the stage itself, and this is a huge stage.

In the new building this utilitarian zone is not confined to the area immediately behind the stage, but extends sideways and forward almost all the way to the Bow Street and Russell Street frontages, and it is high as well, the bulkiest element of the building volume. It is divided into adjacent sections, each bigger than a sea-going container, each capable of being raised or lowered on its own hydraulic supports to facilitate the handling of whole set pieces, and each capable of being moved around. To wander through this area is to be astray in a vast industrial landscape, a shed for the construction of submarines or airships, maybe. As in the master criminal's control centre in a James Bond movie, it seems to be the product of sheer fantasy, since it exists only to generate a fugitive enjoyment in an audience. It is astonishing to see, yet if one didn't set out to find it, its presence would escape notice. This high volume has been surreptitiously threaded through the core of the building, a necessary principle of its organisation, but it needn't trouble you on the night.

Almost as demanding were the requirements of the ballet company. The four practice rooms are arranged in a line directly behind the Floral Hall, at high level so that they can have rooflights, and there are two large studios tucked into the back-stage area on the west side. Add in capacious storage for the extensive wardrobe repertoire, and you are almost back to the scale of industrial provision.

The long-running saga of the opera house has been all too well ventilated in the press over the years, and the waywardness of the committees must clearly have compounded problems for the architects; but even without that aspect of things, one has to marvel at the intricacy of the functional requirements that had to be coordinated. In one way, the project was constrained and simplified by the need to reuse existing facilities, in another way complicated by the impossibility of starting with a *tabula rasa* and an ideal layout. The result lacks the simplicity of Garnier's parti, and succeeds on an entirely different level. We might say that it epitomises Venturi's concept of the duty towards the difficult whole. The whole that it suggests is not the finite balance of the work of art, more like the shifting complexity of the city to which its various parts are related. It is a solution for now.

The elements of this six-sided building which appear on the street are: the nearly symmetrical north elevation to Floral Street, beginning left with Barry's portico and incorporating at its centre the mass of the fly tower and then to the right, the original rear addition, renovated by Gollins, Melvin and Ward in 1982 with remarkable consistency of style; rounding the corner, the projection of this volume on to James Street corresponds satisfactorily to the fly tower behind and above, before we come to the transition to the new construction, and the opening to the new colonnade; next, the two-sided colonnade facing south and west on to the market square; then the administrative spaces facing south on to Russell Street; and finally the series of distinct pavilions facing Bow Street— new facilities incorporating first the truck entry (the only thing that gives a hint of the industrial scale of the scenery landscape), then the restored Floral Hall, and finally the refurbished mass of Barry's porticoed temple. As you might expect, there is a main entry on axis beneath the portico, but there is another main entry in the angle of the colonnade to the square, exactly where the very first theatre entrance was. In terms of modern congestion, both are clearly necessary. From that second entry, in summer, a glimpse of daylight towards the east indicates the direction of the social space, and conversely, it is towards that outlet from the square that the main approach from Bow Street converges eventually. There is no outright axis here, but rather the public foyer system has been sinuously threaded through the building with the same precision as the scenery system.

The reconstruction of a quarter of Inigo Jones' piazza is in itself a significant step. A single act of building thereby contributes towards the re-invention of an important city space, lending itself to field as much as to figure. The colonnades contain shops, reversing the tendency of large buildings to turn their backs on the street and obliterate street activities. The embrace of public space recurs at roof level, where a second colonnade provides terraces for strolling and taking coffee, and for looking back at the city and its spires, Nelson's Column and all, vastly improving the enjoyment of the intervals. The form of the piazza thus provides something like the garden terrace of the classic country house, a destination to balance the formality of the main entrance, and the orientation to south and west reinforces the idea of *détente*.

The entrance level is joined to this upper foyer by staircases, but above all by escalator. The escalator provides the easy way up for those headed for the gods, and brings to an end the more or less shameful ascent via back stairs that used to be the only access for impecunious youth. This is another case of a separate system being threaded through the whole, but this time the escalator is visible to the foyer, and the two ideas offset each other. Now the privileged destined for the front stalls can survey the populace who will share the show, as they rise into prominence; and vice versa, the élite are under the scrutiny of the masses. The escalator defines the edge of the Floral Hall, from whose closed volume, however, it escapes. The Floral Hall, truncated by the demands of the secret scenery jungle just behind it, is still a generous space, and it has been scrupulously restored to provide the opera with the foyer it deserves. A back wall of mirror glass retrieves some idea of its original appearance, and creates a nice paradox where a high balcony in the new amphitheatre bar penetrates through it into the space, and enables the populace to survey the glitterati below. Used as we are to the hole-in-corner character of English theatre foyers, there is relief that here at last is an acknowledgement of the social enjoyment that expands beyond the confines of the auditorium, so elegantly demonstrated by Garnier.

In one sense, since the Bow Street frontage is dominated by the familiar forms of Floral Hall and the Barry portico, it is the colonnaded elevations that serve as the new front to the opera. Here one may note the finesse with which the shop fronts are inserted, the windows rising high in the colonnade while the spaces drop down to fit under the heavy load of necessary accommodation just behind. At the same time, the first row of windows above the colonnade are in fact lunettes which illuminate the peak of the vault. The generous width of the closing opening to the colonnade is managed without excessive height by adopting a four-point arch. The facade above is cleverly handled so as to make an effortless transition from classical piers at ground level to the more basic structure of the roof terrace (although this critic would have preferred a more schematic treatment to come further down). Finally, the change in angle between the wall of the ballet studios and the frontage to the square is marked by a frank *diminuendo* in the lean-to roof to the ballet foyer, which to an architect's eye shows a consoling awareness of contemporary modes.

So we are offered a functionality that goes beyond the physical to include the social. The architects have bent their minds to creating not only the mechanism, but also the amenity, that is appropriate to the operatic tradition, so that London can continue to be classed with Paris and Milan. At least in this respect, we are firmly part of Europe. But, unlike the situation with Garnier, the result is not a single form unified in its expression, but a mixture of measures and a combination of languages.

It could hardly be otherwise with so much already occupying its space and in need of preservation and adaptation. The auditorium itself is retained, but improved and refurbished; the Floral Hall is truncated, but restored to its original appearance; some ancillary areas are renovated and vast new facilities have been added. So it is still possible to exit the stalls through the original entrance foyer and ascend into the grand salon via the original staircase to consume the traditional champagne in familiar surroundings, sheltered by the ancient portico. Or to cross the Floral Hall to the escalator landing and rise up to enjoy the interval in the more modern decor of the new amphitheatre bar, with its views over the rooftops. Bars and fittings have been deliberately moulded to a curvaceous contemporary ideal of relaxation. These are indisputably modern spaces. So this is a building that combines the traditional with the technological, and atavistic pleasures with new ones. But not all in one place. The result is a delicate combination of different things.

It will be criticised by those who need above all to see a direct expression of the artistic unity that is thought to define an architectural statement. It was no problem for

Garnier, active before planners as such existed and before opera houses became dedicated to special effects. With today's demand for specialisation, simplicity only comes with an overwhelming commitment to technological style. This is no problem with railway stations and airports, nor with any programme that can be interpreted as naturally implying the industrial forms that still approximate to our ideal of modernity. That goes up to a point also for art galleries and museums, but it does not necessarily go with retrieving special nineteenth century moments. Neither the auditorium nor the Floral Hall could be rejected, so the *tabula rasa* was not an option. Moreover the special conditions pertaining here have imposed a solution more responsive to the needs of the city block. What the architects have done, however, is altogether more ingenious and civilised, and more sensitive to the place of architecture in the city.

With the National Portrait Gallery, the work envisaged was not visible from the street and was not implicated in ideas of preserving the urban block. It was a discreet and private adjustment that had no identifiable effect on the city at all. The strategy can afford to be more single-minded, but there is the same demand on the architects to integrate places of different character and provenance within an ensemble that has grown over time, and to sew together diverse elements into a coherent experience for the visitor.

Here the whole design follows the perception that building an extension within the light well separating the Portrait Gallery from the adjacent part of the National Gallery would produce little usable space, compared to the use that could be made of the whole of the light well. A deal followed, in which the National Gallery accepted their wall to the light well as a party wall, with no windows and no claims of light, in exchange for a narrow band of rooms in the east wing of the main building fronting St Martin's Place, that would complete the main spaces in the piano nobile within Wilkin's facade. The exchange benefits both galleries, and testifies to the enlightened approach of both directors. The light well is now available not just as a means of bringing down daylight, but as a principle foyer space within the National Portrait Gallery, now leading up to the main suite of top-lit galleries on the top floor, a space that makes sense of the building as a whole. This solution had already been envisaged, and indeed put forward as the preferred option in the presentation made for the competition, which Dixon Jones won in December 1994.

The escalator that takes advantage of the new space makes sense as an effortless way of taking the visitor to the heart of the collection. Charles Saumarez Smith, the director of the National Portrait Gallery, notes that when the project was placed before the Royal Fine Art Commission, there was a hesitation about this: the escalator, it was suggested, was something to do with airports and shopping malls, not with cultural institutions. Good sense prevailed: the general public do not think like that, and in any case flying, shopping and visiting art galleries are increasingly being seen as leisure activities, based on convenience not on duty, the fruit of social maturation in our society, and the very meaning of democracy. Even more than at the Opera, the escalator functions here in a purely architectural way, drawing together a vertically dispersed institution into a kind of vertical concourse and giving it coherence.

The volume in which the escalator rises is itself a triumph of imaginative design, in that the structure supporting the top floor has been condensed into a single column. This makes everything much clearer, and maximises the light falling down through the space. At the top of the escalator, there is a new gallery of Tudor art, long, narrow and rather dark as Tudor spaces often were, its narrowness working for the Mannerist intimacy of the paintings, its length working to distribute the circulation around the top floor. Here, top light has been restored to all the original spaces, giving the maximum amount of conventional display, and making sense of the institution as a national storehouse.

Above the Tudor Gallery is a new restaurant, looking out over a roof landscape to take in a spectacular view of London's skyline to the south and west. The way that this prospect has been combined in sectional design with the necessary windows for the vertical foyer space is typical of the finesse that the architects have shown throughout the project. They have preserved the best of the old, and where necessary extended parts of it to improve its impact (as in the completion of the landing of the original staircase— even to the mosaic floor), and they have eliminated the wilder aberrations, such as the faux-Medieval decor of the entrance lobby from Charing Cross Road: but they have modernised the amenity wherever that was possible, with the aim of bringing the visit together into a coherent experience.

There are certain similarities about both these major projects at a formal level: the seizing of social amenity and the space needed to create it; the careful handling of the old and venerable as entitled to its own share of the action; the bold use of technology where it is helpful, but not as an end in itself; the packing in of all the technical requirements, with the space they need, so that the life of the building is extended as an up-to-date amenity. There is also a certain commonality of theme: in both cases the amenity space at the upper level looks out across an urban roofscape towards the afternoon sun, and is centred on the empowering escalator, bringing a sense of modern amusement to cultural events.

The result in both cases is a carefully balanced whole that does not display all its parts at the same level of noise. Boldness is balanced with discretion, directness of concept is balanced with a mature judgement. This is clearly a conciliatory modern architecture, not a radically subversive one: it is an architecture that aims to serve client and users, and promote the enhancement of life. In this it follows the tradition of modern architecture itself, when it first offered to enhance life through functionality. The achievement in these two projects is tremendous: together they offer exemplary instances of the way that well-loved amenities can be improved and modernised, indeed transformed, without losing their familiar character and their settled place in society.

It is natural to speculate on the future of an architectural partnership that displays such a fine touch. The differences in the partners' approaches may be summarised by the contrast between two of their buildings for Darwin College at Cambridge: the Computer Building and the Residential Building. The first is beautifully fitted into a prominent and difficult site, the second creates its own site from geometry and orientation. Saumarez Smith has surmised that the two partners complement one another in a particularly effective way—they work symbiotically, perhaps—and while they refuse to acknowledge any differences in their approach, their effectiveness may lie precisely in these differences. Jeremy, he says, "sees architecture as a process of subtle adaptation through the process of design", whereas Edward "is more interested in issues of broad outline and concept, in the geometry of the project and [in] retaining its integrity as a modern building".

From what one already knows of the two architects, this judgement from someone who has worked with them seems to be very perceptive. The truth, however, may be more complex, since both are complete architects who can each do everything that needs to be done. In one sense, neither needs the other. But they clearly do work together extremely well, so it may be better to suppose that they share something important, perhaps a direct sense of architecture at the purely intuitional level, an ability to evaluate ideas very fast, to see all the implications of an idea at once. In other words, they share a sense of design.

This is pure speculation. In any case, architecture, unlike other arts, benefits from intimate discussion, from elaborate working out, in the attempt to objectify a hypothesis before it runs away with the design. So at the very least, they must discuss their problems thoroughly. The architect must proceed without the advantage readily available to poet or painter, of simple trial and error, carried out in entire privacy in one's own good time. Errors must be eliminated by the time the design goes through the laborious and expensive process of presentation, specification, management and construction, which in terms of a project like the Royal Opera House, implies a lifetime of sleepless nights.

London, November 2000, Dixon Jones—Buildings and Projects, published Right Angle Publishing, London, November 2002.

Launch of the AD number on *The Tragic* at the Colony Club, guest editor Richard Patterson presides, 27 November.

Memorial service for Ewen Henderson at the Notre Dame Centre near Trafalgar Square, 29 November.

Breakfast at British Museum for opening of central space: Norman's anecdote on Chancellor Schröder, 4 December.

We make belated inspection of the Millennium Dome, lunch at L'Acclaim, Gerbeau seated at next table, 20 December.

We attend Adrian Forty's Inaugural as Professor of History in Darwin Hall, UCL, 5 December.

2001

RM and CS take a break in Paris by Eurostar: Hotel de Nevers; lunch to Terry Farrell, 5/28 January.

We attend a big *at home* by the Barlows in Highgate; Eleanor gets lift home to Cambridge with Horace, 4 February.

Dinner with Mohsen Mostafavi to meet James Ackerman, at the Criterion; others guests are all young.

From their conversation, they seem to be all in showbiz, so all presumably well paid.

RM lectures on Stirling at University of East London for Andrew Higgott, 13 February.

RM and CS to Oostend for her participation in show at MOMA (three heads); last trip in Scirocco, 23–24 February.

Twentieth Century Society visits RM's house in Kennington Park Road, now seen as very 'sixties'.

Norman Foster lectures at the Old Theatre, LSE: slides beautifully managed from computer: PowerPoint, 15 March.

RM buys new car, a Renault Mégane Dynamique Coupé for some £12,000, all saved, 1 May.

RM to Dublin to inspect building by two young architects, one American, one a Dubliner, 10/12 May.

Fingal County Hall
Bucholz McEvoy Architects, 2001

FINGAL COUNTY HALL, DUBLIN
ARTICLE FOR *DOMUS*

Here is a building by an entirely new firm of young architects, partners both professionally and through personal choice: Merritt Bucholz, a Cornell-trained American, and Karen McEvoy, a Dubliner trained at University College Dublin. They met while both were working in New York for Emilio Ambasz. They won the competition in 1996, only a year after Merritt had completed his Masters Degree at Princeton in 1995. They have continued to practise together, during an interim period spent mainly in Paris. The commission was awarded as soon as the competition was judged in 1996. Work started on site in April 1998. To get a building of this size completed within five years they have had recourse to collaboration with an experienced firm—Building Design Partnership in Dublin. It is still a remarkable achievement for them, and it is clear that while they have benefited contractually from BDP experience they have kept a firm hand on the design. It is their own design that has now been built, and it has the fascination of being a practical and successful design from a younger generation, whose education was marked by the uncertainties brought in by the deconstructive revolution. It is almost a relief then to find that, while it is fresh in many ways, it has a basic common sense about it that allows one to hope for the future.

Dublin has been expanding rapidly since the Republic of Ireland joined the European Union. From being originally one of the poorest nations, Ireland has now one of the highest per capita incomes in the Union, and the economic expansion has led to a reorganisation of the administrative zones of the capital into three new counties, beginning in 1992. The County of Fingal occupies the best part of the northern half of the metropolitan area, from the coast westward, and has the added advantage of enclosing Dublin Airport. David O'Connor, the County Architect, was involved in organising the two stage public competition, and he was frank about the fact that the Bucholz-McEvoy design was already preferred amongst all those in the first stage submission, to the extent that he heaved a sigh of relief when it also clearly topped the second stage. It was preferred largely on account of its masterly site plan.

The building presents a clear concave facade to the north end of the main street of Swords, and is set back behind a group of mature trees, a crescent of evergreen oaks and a single Himalayan cedar, whose size matches up to the five-storey building and defines the public space in front of it. It also mediates the transition to the still two-storey shops on the other side, no doubt destined to intensify in time. The landscaping includes lines of slate paving extending out from the building, enclosing gravelled and ivied areas, and making clear the civic nature of this space. To the north are the remains of the superb Norman castle, flanked by the somewhat diminutive Law Courts, with the eleventh century Abbey just beyond. The south end of main street is designated as commercial, and includes an in-town shopping centre, meant to reinforce, and not destroy, the existing amenities. Although for the time being all traffic has to negotiate main street, a relief road is planned. Behind the building, three wings of office accommodation reach out eastwards, enclosing two spaces with distinctive landscaping, one hard, one soft.

The curved facade encloses, along the middle third of its length, a tall atrium, extending up the whole height of the building, and further emphasised by a special section of double-curved roof, supported on cantilevered and strutted steel beams but lined in timber. This atrium space is unusual in that the large panes of plate glass hung from the roof, are given stability by a complex tensile structure of steel wires which tie it back to the main concrete structure, one set curved on plan to match the facade, the other curved in opposite mode to meet the structure of the balconies at either end. The space is thus filled with an assortment of wires, suggesting the life of an aviary, yet offering no obstruction to non-flying humans. Viewed from below, they function rather as a species of decoration, but they do not obstruct the horizontal view outwards from each floor level. At the point of attachment to the glass, there is recourse to a series of wooden spars in laminated American oak (originally referred to as *boomerangs*), each of which supports the panels above and below, and is held by fine pre-stressed vertical cables dropping down close to the glass. These spars use the strength of their pre-stressed supports to secure the glass facade against variable wind strains. They show in their demanding detail how obsessively the architects have followed through the principles of the design, in collaboration with the Peter Rice office in Paris (the structural engineers RFR). Behind, the edge of the floor levels follows and reinforces the curve of the main building, and a series of regular staircases links each floor visibly to the one above, only the lowest of which is wider, corresponding to the link of ground to first floors, where the general public has a right of access. The grand staircase thus takes on a new meaning, being in this case not in the slightest degree monumental, yet integral with a truly grand space.

On these lower levels are situated public counters, waiting areas, a cafe, interview areas, and at the south end, the Council Chamber. On the upper levels are the communal areas serving the offices, with meeting rooms and service cores. The working offices, extending outwards in parallel order, are calm, orderly group spaces, with service rooms at the point of attachment and a few private offices at the outer ends. The environment is controlled by means of natural air flow (only the Council Chamber and a few committee rooms have air-conditioning). The decor has been given a wonderful unity and suavity by strict control of the lighting, all of which is indirect, reflected off glass sheaths. The preponderant colour is grey, but with a pleasing variety of texture and tone. An important element in assuring the comfort of the people working here is by affording them a degree of control over their environment, by means of moveable louvres situated at intervals along the southern face.

The most important single space is the Council Chamber, on the ground floor at the south end. In the original design, the podium in front was occupied by a ramp, but at the client's request this was omitted, and a large window opened up behind it. The view out allows the councillors to momentarily escape their restricted environment, but also allows the people to see what is being done in their name. Where privacy is essential, a series of vertical wooden louvres can be turned to block the view. The focus of the chamber is ensured by two concentric circles of glass-topped desks, the outer one a little higher, each place equipped with reading light and microphone, the whole drawn together by a baldaquin of four columns rising to a ring of flat ceiling. In an asymmetrical volume, these also are arranged irregularly, but the perception is of order and calm. On the inner face, a public gallery looks in; the large outer wall is to be enlivened by a glass sculpture by the Irish artist Vivienne Roche.

The exterior of the building is more variegated than one might expect. This shows not so much in the front elevation as in the detailing of the subsidiary blocks. There is plenty of glass, aluminium window frames and balcony rails, terracotta tiles on the walls of Council Chamber, and, at the north end, the cafe. The concrete appears in places, in an excellent lightish finish, and there are two kinds of metal sheathing, as well as the timber linings to the aerodynamically shaped roof panels which float above the volumes. The vertical ventilating panels (controllable by the inmates) are finished in two colours. The ensemble is brighter and more populist in feeling than the office interiors, which are by contrast austere.

The building as a whole has been extremely popular, much enjoyed by its users. It has elements of a certain audacity—the atrium, with its crowd of slender tensional stiffeners—and elements that everyone can recognise. It feels modern, but is not particularly avant-gardist. Architects will recognise it as fulfilling present-day stylistic requirements, having both High-Tech elements and a kind of relaxed a-formalism. It remains an astonishing achievement for such young architects, designed with devotion, brought to completion with efficiency and verve. It is in tune with the new Irish confidence, and would not surprise if discovered in, say, Strasbourg, since it speaks with conviction of the new Europe.

London, March 2001, published April 2001.

LETTER
TO *ARCHITECTURAL RESEARCH QUARTERLY* ON LESLIE MARTIN

To the Editor, *ARQ*
Dear Sir,

It has been some consolation for the loss of Leslie Martin, a major figure in twentieth century British architecture, to read the special issue of *ARQ* dedicated to his memory. He was a great Englishman, a rare combination of theorist and teacher, of politician and generous benefactor. His retrieved article of 1972, "The Grid as Generator", is a theoretical demonstration of the qualities of the urban grid, and of how it may form the basis for a latter-day return to the problem of controlling urban development. As such it is masterly in its explicative power and in its prescience. And yet it raises some questions as to the role of design in urban design.

The aspect of the grid which is of greatest moment is its neutrality. We may compare the advantages and disadvantages of certain dimensions in the layout, the differences in practice of Chicago and Manhattan as gridded street frameworks. What is important is the way the grid makes a relationship between occupation of the ground by built form and access to it for people and vehicles. Unfortunately, in the coagulated condition of the city today, the only form of large scale intervention allowed is the comprehensive development, in which the public authority makes some kind of deal with a developer looking to make a profit from land values. Even the kind of integration which worked so well in the Rockefeller Center in Manhattan does not seem possible today.

The diagram in which Le Corbusier shows how a comprehensive approach could 'improve' the design of the Manhattan grid, is the point where certain reservations begin to surface. Le Corbusier was a great architect, but his vision of the twentieth century city has been largely a disaster. The city is a cultural artefact, and the model proposed by one man is too reductive to retain the necessary complexity and contradiction without which no city can exist. The city must be the work of many hands and of generations of men. We must therefore be suspicious of any intervention in the grid that creates a different focus and seeks to impose a design pattern that goes beyond the individual building.

The Brunswick Centre, by Patrick Hodgkinson, following on Martin's proposals for the Foundling site, fits well into a street grid, but it does not demonstrate the neutral quality of the grid. It is too much of a design to succeed in this. Its homogeneity isolates it from the street grid and makes it into a megastructure, and as such we almost feel relief that it was left unfinished, because there is already too much of it. It carries with it a loss of gridded street.

The difficulty is not one alone of design. Certain developments in the United States are interesting in showing how a planned layout may encompass streets and building plots, yet both Davis' Seaside and Disney's Celebration are not 'real' places, and their lack of this quality shows how far we have still to go in searching for a new relationship between public ownership and private development to be able to make new places with genuine city characteristics. The work needed is not that of design vision alone, but of a new understanding between architects, engineers and planners. So far the only indication that such an understanding is even desirable comes from the new course in City Planning, Engineering and Architecture set up by Max Steuer at LSE. It will need time to have its impact, but in the meantime it is a fitting place where the search for this new relationship may be pursued and might take shape.

Yours,
Robert Maxwell

London, 25 May 2001, published 2001.

B lectures at Liverpool John Moore's for Brian Hatton, 4/5 June.

Mary Stirling unveils a memorial plaque in the porch of Christ Church Spitalfields, designed by C, 25 June.

We throw a welcome back party for Alan Colquhoun at Mall Studios, 1 July.

We do a one-day trip to Paris; see Rodin, Libera at Pompidou; at end we are exhausted, 14 July.

Rick Mather gives a summer party at the Dulwich Museum: on the walls, some Hodgkins have been introduced, 19 July.

We visit Robert and Fanny's site—a Bofors gun emplacement—in Kent. Barbecue, 18 August.

Visit Barney and Sophie at Sibton; then dinner with Cadbury-Brown and Betty in their very modern house, 24 to 26 August.

Michael Andrews' reception at the Tate Modern; dinner with Alan Powers at Judd Street, 8 September.

Worst act of mass terrorism: World Trade Center destroyed by hijacked jets; 3,000 killed, 11 September.

On TV RM saw a man performing acrobatics on a pole thrust out from one of the towers.

Surprised that he wasn't picked up by any of the subsequent films that were made.

We go to Melinda's concert at the Queen Elizabeth Hall, with Oliver Knussen conducting, 12 October.

RM and CS at La Gaffe for Christmas with Julian and Teresa. On the way back, we visit Marseille, stay at the Unité, take photos on the roof.

The Architectural Forum at the Royal Academy discusses abstraction and representation: RM produces a paper for discussion.

PICASSO AND DUCHAMP
ANALYSED BY DAVID SYLVESTER

David Sylvester in his book *About Modern Art*, 1996, has a chapter on Picasso and Duchamp. Although Picasso was prolific in what he produced, and Duchamp sparing, Sylvester treats them as very much on a par. And it could be said that between them they have virtually dictated the values followed by art in the twentieth century. While he analyses their similarities and differences very closely, Sylvester does not, however, say in one word what distinguishes them.

I do. I think that the force in Picasso was the conflict between representation and abstraction: Picasso dealt in transformations, and he wanted you to be aware of the transformations that had taken place. So, however abstract, Picasso never turns away completely from some level of representation, and the degree of abstraction he employs in any case is part of the meaning of his forms. Duchamp, however, is not concerned with clarifying his meaning, he is content to suggest that there is some meaning there, but he is happy for it to remain a mystery. His idea is to play with the artist's intention, making it rich by obscuring it. He is playing a game with the observer, which he sets up in such a way as always to win. His game is to do with conceptualisation. The idea *behind* what he displays.

Conceptualisation and abstraction are the two primary forces at work in modern art. Abstraction was Picasso's method; conceptualisation was Duchamps's.

> *The time when Picasso was making his first junk sculptures was also the time when Duchamp made his first sculpture from ready-made materials. It was a bicycle wheel placed upside down on a stool. Now, the two objects assembled here are the most basic objects in man's winning dominion over the earth and in distinguishing himself from the beasts of the field: the stool, which enables him to sit down off the ground at a height and a location of his choice; the wheel, which enables him to move himself and his objects around. The stool and the wheel are the origins of civilisation, and Duchamp rendered them both useless. Picasso took junk and turned it into useful objects such as musical instruments; Duchamp took a useful stool and a useful wheel and made them useless... but neither more nor less useless than art is. He turns them into things that are there only to be looked at. Where Picasso seems to be saying that bicycle parts can become sculpture through the force of his personal magic, Duchamp seems to be saying that bicycle parts can become sculpture simply by being treated as sculpture.*

Sylvester, p. 417.

Sylvester points out that halfway through the long gestation of Duchamp's last major work *Étant donnés*, his most complex and ambitious piece of assemblage, Picasso also made an assemblage in the summer of 1956 called *Les Baigneurs*, almost entirely out of bits of wood. It's not so different from earlier wooden constructions, resembling both driftwood and primitive figures. *Étant donnés,* on the other hand, is different in every conceivable way from previous pieces; it is an elaborate piece of staging, it is unique, it is immovable, it occupies a place apart and beyond our reach, and it can be seen by only one person at a time, because it has to be viewed through a peephole. Duchamp keeps us guessing largely by concealing the face of the figure in the installation.

> *Given the modern artist's freedom, Picasso gloried in the possibilities it opened for unconfined and unambiguous self-revelation; Duchamp handed on the freedom to the audience, and with it the uncertainty. The Dionysian and the Apollonian.*

If Sylvester is right about his last point, it goes a long way towards explaining why these two artists between them have been so important in the development of twentieth century art. It also raises some interesting questions as to why these two attitudes have not developed together and in the same way. At the end of the twentieth century, abstraction is faltering, with representation making a comeback, and conceptualisation has begun to take its own way. Discuss conceptualisation with reference to recent developments in art and architecture.

London, October 2001.

Denys Lasdun's Memorial at the Royal College of Physicians; we arrive late, so are in the gallery, 21 October.

RM gives seminar at AA on *Rowe's influence on Stirling*, for Brian Hatton, 28 November.

RM suffers mini-stroke while teaching at AA; Dr Posner prescribes aspirin, 75 mg daily, 13 February.

Lecture at Hayward by Harrison Birtwistle, Melinda on oboe: subject: music and architecture, 7 March.

Starting with: Paul Klee's *Taking a Line for a Walk.*

We attend Sandy Wilson's 80th birthday party at the British Library, 18 March.

We attend Peter Murray's celebration of 25 years in Architecture Club, at Kensington Palace Gardens, 24 May.

RM and CS return to Spencer de Grey's house at Geay, Charente, for a two weeks vacation. This time no fall, no disability, altogether more enjoyable. We are still wowed by immense numbers of hollyhocks in the seaside churchyard in Talmont, July.

To National Portrait Gallery for Ed and Jeremy's book launch; RM has a chapter in it, 25 September.

To Richard MacCormac's house for pre-party, then to Wapping Power Station for his office party, 25 October.

RM speaks at Dennis Sharp's book launch in the AA bookshop: *Visual History of C20 Architecture*, 7 November.

VISUAL HISTORY OF C20 ARCHITECTURE
BOOK LAUNCH
Dennis Sharp, Images 2002

It gives me a lot of pleasure to see the full history of twentieth century architecture launched today. As a teacher of modern architecture, I have had occasion to use *The Visual History* frequently, and often had cause to regret its lack of coverage of the years after 1970. There were three entries for 1970, all contributions to Expo 70 at Osaka; one entry on the Bank of America in San Francisco (by Wurster, Bernardi and Emmons with SOM), and two pictures of the Sydney Opera House, which now gets a full page under 1973–1974. After that, it was no help, which means I have had to manage for 30 years on the slides I could make myself. Now we have the full story, and its much easier to see the twentieth century in its roundedness, even though it seems to go on, in much the same way, under the up-coming title of *Twenty-First Century Architecture*. As the inventor of the genre, I hope that Dennis has made all his arrangements for the coming century, and will not give way to imitators. We look forward to the next book.

    It is instructive to compare the two editions. The main difference is in the judgement of what picture to put at the top of the page to grab the attention. There is a wider knowhow today of where people look first, which I first became aware of when Celia worked for Norman Foster, because it was a prime consideration with him in the production of reports. On the other hand, many of the pages are pretty much the same in both editions, which shows that the editing was already up-to-date for its time.

There is one major omission, which I greatly regret: on pp. 170 and 171 we used to have two great houses, each of which got a full page. Left was Charles Eames' Case Study House, right was Paul Rudolph's Healy Guest House, at Sarasota in Florida, the one with the roof supported on steel straps in a catenary curve. Both are better works than either architect produced later, so I reckon this as a great loss.

The Visual History is not a work of scholarship, exactly, since we have got used to the idea of looking closely at individual architects or separate subjects, which it does not attempt to do. Yet it contributes to scholarship by its rigorous method, because it shows exactly what was built and in what order. Individually written histories have to tell a story, and the author's ideology enters in, making it a bad or a good history. Dennis has his own preferences, for instance, in his interest in Expressionism and so on, but in *The Visual History* he has been very balanced in his judgements, and the result is a book that is factually grounded, and therefore indispensable. I congratulate Dennis Sharp as a discerning author, both as regards his method and his subject. It's hard to see the twenty-first century coming out better.

London, 7 November 2002.

RM and CS to Venice: visit Guggenheim, concert Ca'Razonica, dinner Montin's, 8/11 November.

RM and CS take a few days off at Montpellier, via Marseille: Peugeot 206 from Hertz; RM drives.

We visit Le Grau du Roi, lunch in La Pastourelle, St Martin, where the local wine is Pic Saint-Loup.

As a result of meeting Alix McSweeny, RM starts being invited to write Brief Reviews for the TLS.

ARCHITECTURE: A VERY SHORT INTRODUCTION
BRIEF REVIEW FOR TLS
Architecture: A Very Short Introduction, Andrew Ballantyne, Oxford University Press, 2002

Architecture like most subjects that define a major human activity, has a vast extent, and Andrew Ballantyne has done his share in extending it, by a recent book he edited that made no nonsense about adding to its physical core a phenomenological aura. Paradoxically, this approach has also given him a means of reducing it, to bring it into the framework of Oxford's series of very short introductions. He does this by treating it as a subject open to culture, and definable only within culture.

The most common framework for any history is a chronological one, and Ballantyne acknowledges this by an appendix he calls "Timeline", which starts with the first pyramid at Zoser, and ends with the Guggenheim at Bilbao. Otherwise his examples are arranged in a much freer way by being organised into three chapters: "Buildings have meaning", "Growth of the Western tradition", and "How buildings become great". The central one is chronological in following the story of the temple, from the Parthenon through Chartres and Bourges, the pilgrimage chapel of Wieskirche, Jefferson's Monticello, then back to the Pantheon and the Maison Carrée before taking in Palladio and Lord Burlington, by which time the temple has become more phenomenological, and the past as an aspect of memory has taken on a more generic meaning.

The problem is, then, to discuss architecture within a personal framework that will be thoroughly familiar to most people. He starts with the idea of home and the contrast between the familiar and the unfamiliar, and goes on to consider local landmarks and national monuments, and the play of reason in the processes of conviction and seduction. There are a few uncomfortable moments, for example when we are required to acknowledge the supremacy of past *élitism* in a future that may be evolving towards a more democratic future, but on the whole the line holds, and architecture is made more approachable, if it still remains distant. It is a pity that the illustrations, which are cunningly chosen, are so dismally reproduced.

London, November 2002, published Times Literary Supplement, 17 January 2002.

LOOKING AROUND
BRIEF REVIEW FOR *TLS*
Looking Around, Witold Rybczynski, Scribner, 2002

This is a book of essays written for different publications and different occasions over a five-year period (1986–1991). It was published in the United States in 1992, and comes out now in Britain some ten years later. This delay results in some loss of topicality, particularly felt in the concluding line of each piece, which sometimes assumes a predictive note. The future has continued to emerge and develop, independent of the author's predictions. But this doesn't matter much; what tells is the way that everyday values are slotted into a historical narrative, furnished with names and dates. As for the roving eye, the comparison is probably with Reyner Banham, and some of the titles are certainly Banhamesque, as "Hot Housing Buttons" or "Low-Cost Classicism".

Rybczynski teaches at McGill, and the didactic nature of his writing comes through. Writing for a North American public, he knows that the context cannot be taken for granted. In "Looking Back to the Future" he sketches with a masterful concision the social background of the mid-Victorian family house, before theme parks and automobiles, when people entertained themselves at home. "Getting Away from It All" is a reprise of Palladio's service to the Venetian aristocracy through building cheap farms that were gorgeously grand and architectural, a story originally told by James Ackerman. Rybczynski brings this alive for the ordinary reader, and incidentally explains why Palladio has continued to be an enormous influence even today.

One is gradually brought to accept the design philosophy behind all this, which unlike that of Banham is thoroughly conservative. He clearly approves of Modernists like Moshe Safdie and Renzo Piano, but also postmodernists like Peter Rose and James Stirling. He can see the good in Robert Davis' Seaside, Léon Krier's Poundbury, and Michael Graves' Portland Building, which more ideological Modernists are unable to tolerate. He prefers his new office within what was built as a chemistry lab in 1896 to the old one in the building constructed for architecture in 1958. His judgement is based on common sense, rather than avant-garde hype. The result is often enlightening, and in the critic, this is no bad thing.

London, November 2002, published 6 December 2002.

2003

We find that red Pic St. Loup can be had at Safe Ways: RM buys 6 bottles, and many more, 2 January

It turns out this supply lasts exactly a year, then dries up

Receive invitation to Pierre von Meiss giving his *Leçon d'Honneur* at Lausanne on 19 March next: send regrets

ARCHITECTURAL REFLECTIONS
BRIEF REVIEW FOR *TLS*
Colin St John Wilson, Manchester University Press 2001

This book has been reissued after a lapse of eight years. In the meantime, as Roger Stonehouse points out in his preface, Wilson's reputation as an architect has changed through public experience of his *opus maximus* The British Library. (It reminded Prince Charles of a Police Academy.) From being reviled he is now praised, the Library is seen by its users as both comfortable and supportive. Wilson's theoretical position is unchanged: in an unusual occurrence, the appreciation of his practical work has led to a fresh demand for his theory.

Wilson's song is a reiteration of functionalism. Yet he takes a position that is probably unfamiliar to a British public hugely influenced by the late Reyner Banham's praise for the factually grounded. Wilson applauds the architect's search for functional truth, but does not renounce his search for appropriate expression. In doing this he bases himself on a tradition rather than on a simple polemic; a tradition based on the works of architects like Scharoun and Aalto, where, he claims, neither form nor content is unduly privileged.

His ideas are integrated into a philosophical discussion of the human condition, and he is totally aware of certain attendant ambiguities. He rejects the brusque calls to action of naive functionalists like Hannes Meyer, and respects the achievements of the literary modernists Joyce and Eliot, along with the reflections of more ambiguous figures like Loos and Wittgenstein. He also rejects the "sacred games" of the aesthetes, the enigmas of Duchamp and de Chirico. Meaning, in architecture, must be grounded in use: but it cannot automatically follow function.

He thus opens up the need for a certain responsibility in the architect: he must express himself, yes, but not at the expense of the public values that architecture is expected to embody. This is to lay emphasis on the ethics of architecture. In avoiding the glib determinism of High-Tech and the excesses of self-expression, Wilson recalls architecture to a sense of its public duty. Paradoxically, his ideas will be reassessed by his own powers of self-expression.

London, February 2001, published Times Literary Supplement, 23 December 2001.

TRACING ARCHITECTURE
BRIEF REVIEW FOR *TLS*
Edited by Dana Arnold and Stephen Bending, Blackwell, 2003

Here is a book that calls for ample illustration, and gets by with a bare minimum. It deals with the period when published engravings of monuments began to have an impact on architectural taste, providing a visual input to go along with the verbal, a moment which happens to correspond with Winckelmann's impact on art criticism. His *Monumenti antichi inediti*, published in 1767, replete with engravings, revolutionised the understanding of art history. The visual evidence improved the authority of the text, in spite of the fact that the plates were "notoriously inaccurate and pathetically unattractive".

In her introductory article on "Facts or Fragments", Arnold has benefited from showing us photographs of the Greek temples at Paestum, and this helps us to understand the gap between two kinds of plates: measured drawings, which conform to a broadly scientific approach, and picturesque views, like those by Piranesi, which contributed enormously to the public assimilation of visual history. Her co-editor Stephen Bending has just two illustrations, both dealing with the work of Francis Grose, whose *Antiquities of England and Wales*, together with Andrew Hogg's plagiarised edition of it, demonstrate this process of popularisation. To a plate of Lindisfarne, Hogg has added some extraneous Gothic detail, two antiquaries examining a tomb, and a distant view of Stonehenge, without clearly leaving the world of fact for fiction.

The most interesting essay is that by Susan Dixon, who compares Piranesi's use of "multi-informational" plates, in which different aspects are combined in a single engraving, with a similar usage made by Houël in his *Voyage pittoresque* of 1782. We come to appreciate the importance of the image. Abigail Harrison Moore shows the importance of Denon's Egyptian images in creating Napoleon's myth of Ancient Egypt, and Andrew Ballantyne in his discussion of *Imperialism and the Decline of Art*, shows how Richard Payne Knight made effective use of engravings without fully understanding the provenance of his examples.

This little volume leans towards a certain antiquarianism, but it does deal with a typical shift towards modernity, where a loss of authenticity is balanced by a gain in accessibility.

London, 8 July 2003, published 1 August 2003.

After receiving an email from Mark Cousins, RM agrees to teach History of Modern Architecture at the AA, January.

RM joins an AA trip to Bordeaux, sees Rogers' Law Courts, the Koolhaas Villa, Pessac, Arcachon, 24 to 28 April.

On return trip RM has good chat with Monica Pidgeon, who promises to invite us to her place in Highgate.

RM visits Tony Fretton's house for a member of the Sainsbury family in Chelsea, and agrees to review it for *Casabella*.

A HOUSE IN CHELSEA FOR AN ART COLLECTOR
CASABELLA

Last year we were visiting some friends of my wife who live in a typical English Palladian country house, built in brick around 1830. They took us to see another Palladian house in the neighbourhood, which was not in the English tradition of Palladio, but was actually by Palladio. It was a replica of the Villa Caldogno, not to be found in the *Quattro Libri*, admittedly, but a close relative of the Villa Saraceno, which is. There it was, built with archaeological exactitude, standing in rural Nottinghamshire, as authentic as if you had found it in the Veneto. Although it is one of Palladio's more modest designs, what strikes you on seeing it in an English context is the generous scale and the magnificence of the internal space.

A very similar feeling of being confronted with something important struck me on visiting this house in Chelsea. It's not a country villa, of course, but a town house, and it fits modestly enough with its neighbours, but it does have the property of being generous. The living room is a wide two-storey high space, which has been designed as a single entity with the aim of providing a setting for large modern works of art. These already look at home in this setting. In Corbusier's Maison Cook there is one part that runs up through two storeys, but only in the very restricted way that he allows void to appear as a combination of two levels within the theory of the free plan, organised horizontally. Here the feeling is quite different, more fundamental, a feeling of being in touch with a well known tradition, somewhat as we find it in the Villa Malaparte. Yet the house is clearly modern in feeling, and intended to be so.

This living room combines a due formality with a sense of informality. In addition to one lateral window on the north wall, there are two windows on each of the front and back walls, facing east and west, and three of these set up a symmetry which is putatively classical. But the fourth, on the street side, is offset and different. It provides an alcove from which an intimate view of the street can be had, or a glimpse of whoever is ringing the door bell, and it breaks the symmetry. Viewed from the outside, the volume of this alcove forms a projection central to the mass of the house, the focus of the facade, somewhat as we find it in Le Corbusier's Maison Planeix or in Adolf Loos' Möller House. Although the windows to either side are asymmetrically disposed, the emphasis on the axis is reinforced by the large sliding doors to the double garage below, centrally located, and faced in the same stone as the rest of the facade.

In the living room a fireplace in the centre of one lateral wall reinforces the general formality, but the staircase on the opposite wall which runs down to the dining room introduces the notion of a private passage to the festivities, and this brings us back abruptly to the present. In addition, the plaster ceiling is gently modulated by a series of wave forms, asymmetrically disposed in plan, which help the wall lighting and also substitute in a way for a more traditional effect. So there are strong elements of the design that work together to make a unique interior, special to this house, without having to declare allegiance to any of the received ideas of today. It is ideologically released. The feeling that it engenders is one of being free from dogma, but at the cutting edge of a new beauty. It's a good feeling.

Taking the stairs down to the act of dining, one arrives in a glass pavilion, projecting entirely into the rear garden, surrounded by plants. The planting provides the wallpaper, somewhat as in the Tugendhat House. In season, one can take a brief turn in the open air. The space is filled by the dining table, and is concentrated on the dinner conversation. After dark, one is mildly distracted by glimpses in the plate glass of oneself talking, It's like being in a private restaurant. The act of dining is dramatised and one's sense of life being sweet is reinforced.

The same feeling attaches to the library. This occupies a level equivalent to the upper part of the living room, and is approached from a landing half way up the main staircase that leads to the bedroom floor. Easy to miss altogether, this room creates for itself a special intimacy. The library runs from front to back and has a window on both facades, and a sitting area towards the centre for exchanging confidences. The inner wall is lined with books. So it is both an impressive space and a very private one, more or less tucked away from public view: an unusual feeling, and a clever piece of planning.

The bedroom floor is also unusual, in that the guest bedroom and the spare bedroom on one side are separated from the master bedroom on the other by a hothouse containing tropical plants and a winter garden, which together occupy the middle zone, so that privacy between host and guests is very thorough. This separation is effected by planting, and plants being in the realm of nature, discretion is total. There is at the same time the excitement of sharing, if invited, the external hot tub on the roof garden, or at least the sense of intimacy created by its mere presence. So the house as a whole enters into the game of entertaining one's guests, or of being privileged by one's host. Together, the way the spaces of this house are organised makes an effective game out of the idea of enjoying social space. It is not exactly the house as *une machine à habiter*, more as *un endroit à faire plaisir*.

In one sense it may be taken as a modern version of the classical town house, the very type invented by Palladio at the Casa Cogollo, Vicenza. That is quite modest, especially when compared to the various *palazzi* there, all of which confirm the concept of grandeur by which aristocrats originally lived in town, and this gives it an almost modern feeling, like a do-it-yourself *palazzo*. The use here in Chelsea of stone facing, and of individual windows, door sized or smaller (except for the concealed dining pavilion), strengthens the feeling of a traditional town house, and ensures that it fits quietly into the neighbourhood. Yet this effect comes from its organisation and interior meaning, it is not the result of a scenographic presentation betraying the mode of being built for effect. This is what gives one the impression of confronting in Fretton a fresh vision in architecture, a vision that has the inner strength to benefit from traditional achievements without slavishly imitating anything; and to give some freedom to his collaborator Mark Pimlott, responsible for the ceiling in the salon, the pattern in the hall floor, the main stair balustrade and the twin washbasins in the bathroom.

The same independence is visible in the details. The entrance hall has a chrome handrail that begins its ascent with an upward curve, fulfilling the role of grand staircase. Yet it continues its journey without further flourish. The oval pattern in the stone paving is centralised in the space, but turned to a slight angle with the walls and cut off by them in a way recommended by Robert Venturi ("the duty towards the difficult whole") but it does not produce a Venturi 'effect'. The twin washbasins in the principal bathroom are made from a single casting of transparent perspex, while the appurtenances of body care are concealed in the cupboard. The effect is minimalist, but not obsessively so. The bathroom floor is sparsely decorated with lines of coloured mosaic, but it doesn't look decorated. The hot house in the roof garden is harboured in a squarish construction of plate glass supported on an internal metal frame, which makes an effective centrepiece to the garden elevation, but it seems to come out of a study of rainwater flow and structural stiffness, not from a purely decorative intention. The hot tub is carefully managed with a Japanese thoroughness that suggests cleanliness is truly next to godliness. The interiors generally are entirely consistent with the detailing of the exterior. The external cladding is in stone, which lends gravitas, and the red colour ties the house to the brickwork of other houses in the area. There is a discipline in these details that seems to come from a process of inward concentration, not from attention to surface effect.

The volume of the hot house appears on the garden facade with the precision of a cupola on a classical villa, but it also combines with the continuous glazing of the bedroom floor just under it to create a modern feeling for the house, and to express on the outside the private quality of the bedrooms. The glazing masses combine to set off the fairly large expanses of stone below, and the glazed balcony which projects at first floor level across the whole width of the house is identical in its detail with the balcony of the bedroom floor and restates this theme in a gentler way, without reinstating the glazed volume. On the street side, there is no similar play with glass, the red stone takes on a prime importance, and the only hint of the lighter rear character lies in the light stone trim to the bedroom volumes. One is glazed towards the street, the other—the bathroom— is glazed on the south face towards the roof garden, but blank to the street. Both stones are from France, the red one is Guinet Derriaz, the other Buxy Bayadere. Looking upwards, it is the blank area of the red stone that defines the mass of the house, whereas at the rear, it is the glazed volumes that do the same job.

All these materials combine in a wonderful way to give the house an inner coherence, a sense of rightness in the relation of part to whole. There is a formality in the relation of house to street, marked not only by the choice of materials and by scale, but also by the general form. We are governed by near symmetry, but not by absolute symmetry. The separate volumes on the bedroom level balance each other, but are different. The flue outlet acts as a marker of the central axis, but is not in dead centre. The entrance door is set to one side near the party wall in the manner of countless Georgian terrace houses, a functional advantage in practical terms, but it is another level of thinking altogether that brings the double garage into the axial position on centre, disguised by the stone facing on the sliding doors. The garage, indeed, is a fully decorated space, an acknowledged part of the house rather than a utility room, and placed thus on centre and in combination with electronic controls, allows the owner to enter his house en auto with enjoyable panache, and proceed immediately to the grand staircase, whether or not accompanied by his guests.

What we have to recognise here is a reinvestment of the functionalism that inspired the idea of modernity. That form should follow function is written into the rules of modernity. But it does not follow that every item has a fixed value under functional assessment; rather, that the concept of the plan and its subdivisions should correspond to an overall analysis of the client's needs and aspirations. The style of this house is still impregnated with a functionalist rectitude, but it is not due to a particular choice of forms as looking functional; the choice of what Venturi called the industrial aesthetic. Rather we see the function followed as a whole.

All this adds up to a certain *joie de vivre*. This house is clearly meant to be enjoyable to use, to fulfil the owner's social requirements at all levels. Modernism in the home has previously concentrated on fresh air and health, as with the Lovell Beach House by Schindler; or it has picked on kitchen and bathroom, where the modern fitments that replaced servants require a certain precision of the kind that attaches to laboratory equipment, and do something to fill out the concept of *une machine à habiter*. But there is still a big part of living that benefits from a more relaxed attitude towards life. Where the client has the means to enjoy this, he is surely entitled to have it. It has always impressed me that Adolf Loos, in designing his wife's bedroom, had the idea of carrying the white carpet some way up the wall, to express the sweet enjoyment of *détente*, the freedom of privacy. In this house in Chelsea we witness a similar sense of luxury, even a return of humanity, an acknowledgement of our desires as much as of our requirements. Given the ideological commitment of all new architecture to functionalism, this change is liberating. It is a small step for mankind, but quite a big step for architecture.

London, October 2002, published April 2003.

Three days in Paris at Hotel De Nevers: Modigliani, Barthes, Dix, Magritte; dinner with Françoise Choay.

Celia spends a week with Martin at his new flat in Aix-en-Provence, he gives her the key, March.

C climbs Mont Sainte-Victoire easily, enjoys walking with his friends, is a credit to the Scotts.

RM does summing up chair in *Selfhood* conference convened by Jules Lubbock at British Academy, 23 May.

Micky Hawkes asks RM to play background music for an auction of drawings at the AA; he does. It turns out the suggestion was made by Kenneth Powell: it goes well; it's becoming known that he plays, roughly, à la Fats Waller.

We go to *Lohengrin* at Covent Garden. Peter Smithson dies, 7 June.

Cedric Price dies. Obituary in Independent by Kenneth Powell; maybe it's the end of an era, 10 August.

The era that's ending is my generation: most of my old friends have gone, Groak, Boyarsky, Banham, Rowe.

Michael Brawne dies; several obituaries; definitely it's the end of an era.

RM after reading MPhil paper by Irina Davidovici, recasts his AA course to bring in Rowe and Mannerism.

Jonathan Woolf asks B to review a house in Hampstead: *The Brick Leaf House*; it appears in *Architecture Today*.

RM visits the Woolf house in Hampstead: is impressed by the combination of minimalism and luxury.

It reminds him of the first lecture he ever gave: as a student in his third year at Liverpool, he lectured on *Utility and Luxury in Le Corbusier*: the beginning of an interest in dialectics.

DOUBLE HOUSE IN HAMPSTEAD
JONATHAN WOOLF ARCHITECTS:
REVIEW PUBLISHED IN *ARCHITECTURE TODAY*

The world here is privileged, discreet, an area of large conventional houses, well planted and beautifully maintained. The gardens butt on to Hampstead Heath extension, marked by an iron railing, but so thickly wooded that from here it seems like the back of beyond. To arrive at these railings on the public side will put you into instant exposure, looking in on a space of privacy and seclusion, also well planted and about to be beautifully maintained, if not conventional in the normal sense. These houses are unashamedly modern, but with discretion. Each garden is dominated by large mature trees—a copper beech, an oak—that have been here for aeons. The effect is of a clearing in the forest, quite paradisiacal.

The single building consists of two houses, each square on plan, each built around a light well which is normally roofed to make a two-storey internal atrium, adjoining the

Double House in Hampstead
Jonathan Woolf Architects, 2005

staircase. The roof lights, at the touch of a switch, withdraw, so that the cool night air can flood the building. Back in place, they resist the hot air of daytime, or keep out the rain. The plan is climate sensitive, but it employs no sunshades, gaps or gimmicks, and there are no curves. It is the poetry of the right angle, again. Except that there is a gentle oblique angle between the two units, in plan, and a recess that marks the entry of one.

This building provides a home for two brothers and their families, each house being autonomous. The two are however connected by a passage way which can be thrown open to allow parties to surge from one to the other, or left closed up and unnoticed as a sort of family secret. Almost as secret is the way down to the shared swimming pool that lies under the upper house. It is not flooded with light, but top-lit from either end. At one end is a light well that helps to insulate one house from the other; it is plastered in dark cement so that the light is not amplified, but all the same remains as a goal for the swimmer. At the other end a modest topflight inserted in the garden terrace will permit not only light, on occasions, sunlight, to act as a goal for swimming in the other direction. Each length thus has its individual character, an encouragement for the swimmer to go for one more length.

The planning follows the same degree of understatement. The internal atria spread light throughout each house, without impinging on the individual rooms. These all focus on the large windows that admit views of the beautiful garden, without imposing a single orientation. Indeed, it is one of the charms of the house that the hierarchy of rooms is not dominated by one orientation; the lower house opens to the south and east, the upper house to the west and south. The individual rooms are in a sense free from constraint, each ordains in turn its own world.

On the outside, there is a corresponding ambiguity about the hierarchy of the space. The pattern of windows in each wall is strong and well considered, but not regimented. The metal frames are set close to the wall surface, maintaining the plane of the wall, which allows them to be big without disrupting the planes. There is no dominant window wall. The house is thus broken up into episodes. To counter deliquescence, however, detail becomes important. Unity is maintained by the strict control of the detailing, which follows a minimalist style in the sense that it is always direct and consistent, with nothing extraneous. Flooring is always in the same *pietra serena* stone from Florence, and the wood floors and doors are always in American walnut, the handrails in bronze. So the unity of the whole turns out to be a difficult whole, not deriving from a spatial unity, but from a consistency of approach. It remains in place, is even very strong.

To some extent this strategy has developed from the issue of maintaining the autonomy of each house. The architect was conscious of the problems that might emerge in adapting the room divisions to individual requirements, and to allow clients' wishes to be followed through the design period. Partly to keep from possible entanglements during design the structure chosen is a steel frame, concealed in the pattern of partitions, but offering the least opposition to changes that might develop. The absence of a distinct structure and thus of a structural hierarchy is another feature that encourages the sense of being free from an architect's rule.

On the other hand, the rather free pattern of windows on the east, west and south sides is balanced by an almost complete absence of windows on the north or entrance side.

In a way, this has come about because it was considered as a kind of back, while the other sides share their function as front. The sheer walls around the entrance point establish a sculptural quality, intensified by the choice of a handmade Gloucester brick, whose varied texture animates the surface in a telling way. The same brick is used to enclose the garden and outbuilding of the lower house, the one that is nearest the approach, so that the visitor is dominated by the privacy of the enclave, and by the sense of exclusion. The presence of the modest entrance doors within this austere composition renders them doubly hospitable. At the same time, the gentle angle between the two houses softens the composition, gives it a touch of the picturesque without imposing too much.

Another thing that helps to provide variety between the two houses is the presence of the outbuilding, the walls of which also extend the brick enclave approached by the visitor. This contains the garage, a workshop, and a ceramic studio, arranged in a single line. This building encloses the garden for the lower house, the one dominated by a large beech tree, and acts as a support for the building as a whole. The presence of an outbuilding, housing potentially noisy activities, is part of a strategy that the architect has formulated, partly as a response to the empirical requirements, partly as a counterbalance to the formality of the brick sculptural entity, and partly to establish the concept of a 'grand house'. He has issued a short paper called "Notes on Making a Grand House", which makes his intentions clear.

What is at issue here, then, is to develop the concept of the grand house. The double client helps in this, providing a double occasion and double the response. The issue is how to respond without too much revealing the separateness of the double programme, and how to impose an overall unity that doesn't jar. To do this the architect has adopted a strategy of going for a dispersed pattern, avoiding grandiosity as far as possible. I feel that he has succeeded admirably in doing this. It works for the clients, and it works for the public.

There is a general problem about grandeur, which as an aim is far from acceptable in our day and age. It sets individual ownership against the public realm, so it could raise democratic hackles. Long gone is the acceptance of the squire's superiority, let alone the intrusion of a new neighbour. The planners had no difficulty: they wanted above all to maintain the conformity of the development, in this case to keep up the context of a privileged realm: the building had to fit with a neighbourhood of fairly grand houses. The use of a dispersed window pattern, with no intrusion of an overcalled episode on the facade, helped to gain acceptance, no doubt. The choice of brick was safe, as was the use of white window frames, even if metal ones. Yet the house, as a whole, is not conformist, but remains strictly within a Modernist canon.

But it is Modernism with a difference. It uses abstraction, with neat, even slick surfaces; it uses modern construction, using a steel structure not as a matter of faith, but as a practical convenience; compact planning, not for cheapness, but to further the amenity, even the luxury of the programme; environmental principles, but not as an overreaching justification for the parti. It is a different modern building that results.

As one of an older generation that used to think Corbu had the final answer, I am constantly having to revise my ideas since the beginning of the twenty-first century. Nowadays we have had to get accustomed to a new kind of Expressionism, a kind of no-holds-barred radicalism, affected to a large extent by the conceptualism of contemporary art. What matters with Libeskind is his narrative, with Hadid is her unbridled dynamism, with Koolhaas is his surrealism. With Woolf we have a clear originality that eschews any overriding ideology, but for all its understatement projects a hidden strength. It's a quality that I feel grateful for.

London, 20 October 2003, published Architecture Today, November 2003, and Casabella, May 2004.

King post truss settles by a quarter inch, needs attention, says Paul Bell, October.

Work done to king post truss without the need for a scaffold tower, 11 November.

We go to Nice for a break, since we had no real summer holiday; stay in Hotel Grimaldi and enjoy it, 11 to 14 October.

Visit the Musée Matisse, Musée d'Art Moderne, Maeght Gallery; and C has a swim.

Office party by Allies and Morrison, on moving into their new building at 85 Southwark St, 18 November.

RM to Lincoln to view Rick Mather's new School of Architecture; visits Lincoln Cathedral, 1 December.

SCHOOL OF ARCHITECTURE AT LINCOLN UNIVERSITY
RICK MATHER ARCHITECTS:
REVIEW PUBLISHED IN *ARCHITECTURE TODAY*

The day set to visit Lincoln turned out wet and miserable, and the University campus was looking like a prime example of the wetlands, which it is. The persistent rain didn't help the existing new campus buildings, mainly by RMJM, to look like a new start: they had lots of detail, including various panels of brickwork, clearly chosen to match the industrial buildings which are being renovated to provide the new library, and sharing therefore in the damp look. In the middle stood an all white building that stayed white through the rain and gave some hope of better weather to come: the new architecture school by Rick Mather Architects.

One could imagine the first visit to the site by an architect newly commissioned to provide a masterplan: the initial depression followed by the realisation that with so much glub there would be little difficulty in suggesting improvement. Mather's masterplan will use peripheral buildings to exclude the doleful view to the supermarkets on the west, enlarging the site and its landscaped domain, providing new parking under trees, and focussing on a pond formed by cleaning up the balancing excavation which keeps the water table stable in relation to Brayford pool. In addition there will be a second Mather building, recently won in competition—the Lincoln Arts Centre—which will form a square together with the Architecture School. This square will be a meeting place between Town and Gown. The masterplan also envisages new pedestrian links to the High Street, which leads uphill through the town centre, and beyond, to Lincoln Cathedral, the second largest Gothic cathedral in the land (after York). In addition, there is talk of putting the railway which borders the campus into a tunnel, a step which might be expensive as well as reducing the alertness required of students.

So we come to the architecture school itself: white outside and inside, therefore clearly modern. Not the new modernity of metal skin stretched over nondescript structure, but the traditional modern that seeks to provide functionality along with economy. The building will hardly bring the tourists to Lincoln as Gehry's Guggenheim does to Bilbao, but the campus, when complete, will very likely bring students to a congenial university. As a campus it will have all the benefits of York but with improved closeness to the city as an amenity, a sense of urban enclosure set in the middle of the countryside. And the architect has been conscious of the importance of the Cathedral, and has worked to make its presence register on the daily life of the students below. Clearly, this building has been designed with economy in mind. It cost £7.9 million, and was built in just 14 months. Collaboration between the architects and Nigel Stevenson, the project manager, has been exemplary. The University has been won over, and a fruitful partnership engaged.

More importantly, one can say that the search for economy has resulted in benefit. The school is a simple rectangular shed on a concrete frame, with access off two parallel corridors. The space between the corridors has been expanded into an atrium that rises the full height of the building and pulls light down from above, but only at one end of the building. But this atrium ends not in a glass roof, the cliché of our times, but in a series of skylights and clerestory windows. The light that comes down is not blinding, but filtered and reflected off the many white surfaces so that it has a magic quality of increasing the sense of spaciousness. And it does this without using up the budget. The space has been expanded by careful design, won by subjecting the brief to rigorous criticism.

The space of the entrance hall, for example, has been combined with the base of the atrium and the adjoining cafeteria to become the social centre of the building. It also provides the foyer to the two auditoria (one for 250, one for 120) and the performance space at the west end of the building. The social spaces together form a sort of head to the animal, and this not only animates the building, but the plan also. The auditoria are part of a game that puts into play angles that break the conscious rectangularity of the whole, and give a character to the end of the building that faces the high street.

These angles derive in the first place from the shapes of the auditoria. This is extended by slightly revolving them in relation to the axes of the main accommodation, accentuated by the glazing at the entrance. These changes are quite slight in the project as a whole, but they galvanise the volumes, and allow a constrained expression to come through.

The climax of this movement is seen in the view north past the east end, looking to Lincoln Cathedral beyond. This opening forms a window through which campus and cathedral are joined. In sunlight the shadow of the overhanging top floor comes to an exquisite point exactly on the southeast corner, which thus runs uninterrupted to the top of the building. It must have been a great satisfaction when the contractor achieved this alignment without any trouble, and without fuss. This precision only shows because the form of the building is presented as an act of will by the architect, and is the reason for the decision to finish the building in white render. The sculptural effect of the volumes is emphasised by the organisation of the windows into long ribbons that allow the walls to cohere as masses, and to appear as a unified statement.

The same unity of the uniformly white surfaces works inside to tie the atrium together into a single space. Because it has been won by careful planning at each level, it would be destroyed by any variety of finish. The only departure from the white is in the darker grey applied to the two bridges that link north and south corridors; these stand out, but they appear to be insertions that keep the two sides apart, so they also work for the unity of the design as a whole. A similar variation lies in the darker render applied to the plant room on the roof at the western end, which helps to tie in that end of the building and contrast it with the movement simulated by the angles below.

A tour of the building returns one to the discipline of a reduced palate and a rigorous control. The detail is everywhere consistent, and as a result, it vanishes. The main architectural studio on the top floor runs the whole length and is lit by a south-facing clerestory, working with a one way pitched roof. Students from different years are thus sharing space and environment, are conscious of the whole into which they fit. At the east end there is an extensive roof terrace where you can take a break, or down a drink. Because there is, as it were, an absence of detail, there is no fuss, the building becomes the background to work.

The machine shop, so often banished to the basement, here comes up with the water table and takes its place on the ground floor, insulating the performance space from the noise of the passing train. It is well equipped with the latest metalworking equipment, but also gives space to antique woodworking tables from some former place, that in all the surrounding newness take on a surreal animation, as if perpetrated by Max Ernst. They will no doubt prove their usefulness, or go forever.

One further departure from the strict whiteness is found in the reinforced concrete columns that appear on the south elevation. They are finished as smooth concrete cylinders. A couple that carry the loads of the lecture theatres are fatter than the rest, but they hang together as a family. The cement render is applied to the outside of the performance space, so that the building as a whole has the recognisable look of stilted modernity. Elsewhere, the structural loads are absorbed by the walls, or appear as rectangular blocks along the strip windows. The structure is admitted, but not emphasised.

It is, in sum, a discreet building, that works first at being useful, then in looking good. It does not proclaim a unique vision, but it reinterprets modernity in a unique way. It stands clearly for progress, and it deserves to have a bright future. It will combine with a second white building, the projected Lincoln Arts Centre, to start an urban renaissance on campus. The finished campus, if it follows the Mather masterplan, and gets through into a successful landscaped stage, will be a collection of city blocks that will provide a civilised environment.

London, December 2003, published June 2004.

We return to France for a week, with three sunny days of walking in the Calanques, December 2003.

Two days in Bargemon, where we stayed with Mary Stirling in a hotel and inaugurated Ed and Margot's villa.

The villa is simply beautiful: living, terrace, dining and pool *en enfilade*, long colonnade facing south.

HOUSE NEAR BARGEMON, FRANCE
EDWARD AND MARGOT JONES:
REVIEW FOR *ARCHITECTURE TODAY*

I think of this house as a villa, at least partly because it's white walled, like Le Corbusier's villas at Garches and Poissy. The white walls give it an aura of being early modern. Yet, we know, LC was only partly Modernist, he had another side to him that acknowledged the power of process, the process of renewal over time which allowed certain objects to evolve into types, becoming thereby the product of a vernacular tradition. Like the bicycle, or the briar pipe. He saw a historical process that produced a kind of objective achievement. It's possible to see him as torn between an innate classicism and a pull from the future, a tension well documented in Charles Jencks' book *Le Corbusier*, 2000. Because of the way planning controls operate in this part of France, the vernacular tradition is seen as a framework for new construction, as making new construction acceptable, so it was more or less imposed on the architect.

Well, vernacularism has become a sort of dirty word in Britain, where it has similarly been appealed to by planners as a way of ensuring that new development fits in, ever since the 50s when the left wing at the LCC tried to promote 'Voyseyism', Voysey standing for the Arts and Crafts tradition. This has led to a tendency that my daughter has characterised as "institutional nook and cranny". Now there is even controversy about how to build country houses, since the building of country houses was at its most successful during the eighteenth century, and then the only way of fitting in was to be classical.

This tension shows in Edward Jones' design at the point where the main gable wall has been given a horizontal top edge, not showing the slope of the roof behind. The planners objected to this, as an alien marker, that gives too classical a look to the view from the road. But there is hope that with the white being softened to off-white, and the sanding of the house by the wind, this detail will be accepted in the long run. It adds to the interest of a house that otherwise is easily seen as vernacular, simply because it has a mono pitch roof.

But nevertheless, it's not vernacular in one respect: it goes from end to end in a straight line, marked by a row of cylindrical columns, carrying a pergola and defining a front that faces south towards sun and view. This is far from the vernacular play with nook and cranny, which tends to bring in a note of nostalgia and make for something more sentimental. It is, on the contrary, crisp.

Fortunately, the architect could appeal here to the shape of the site, and in particular to the considerable slope from north to south, which makes it difficult to build across the

House near Bargemon
Edward and Margot Jones, 2004

contours. The house very sensibly hugs its contours. So the form of landscape has entered into the design, by imposing a series of bands of reduced width that extends across the whole site. I am reminded of Rem Koolhaas' design for La Villette, which was based on a similar concept, not because of contours, but as a way of achieving contrast.

At least one person I know dislikes it because, she said, it's too straight. For me, that straight line is a condition of the pleasure the house affords.

The 19 bays of its length (giving 20 columns, 19 if you allow for one that has been 'omitted' at the loggia) allow of a very rational subdivision of the plan. Two bays for entrance, two for salon, two for loggia, three for living room (with kitchen) one for loggia, five for swimming pool, four for store room-cum-teenagers-sleepover and terminal ramp. And upstairs, two bays for main bedroom above the salon, then a bridge across the loggia to three bays of guest bedrooms over the living room. It has the neatness of an equation, and it has a rationalist aura.

But this linear equation means that the whole house is directed at the view, and the view is magnificent. Just out of sight is the sea, but you can see this if you walk up the hill behind the house. The sea is the Mediterranean, you are in the south of France. You are living with sunshine, with sunshine every day, with top ingredients for cooking, with a sense of the joy of southern life. The sound of a tinkle on the keyboard won't hurt here, providing it's your own kind of jazz. The barbecue in the loggia plays its part, making you regret that you have become a vegetarian. The day comes to a climax as you sip your drink to the setting sun, waiting for supper, and feeling good about being alive.

The sense of enjoyment in the landscape is reinforced by the garden. We start with the pergola, which in bright sun adds stripes. It will in due course be softened by vines. Then there are plants in tubs, outsize pots that measure up to the grand scale of the architecture; then the vines that are already softening the columns; then the poplars that continue the line of columns towards the west. Then, just below the house, the lawn, which is already a source of interest to the French, who stop for a look (the French, unless checked, put gravel everywhere). I was privileged to see the lawn being sewn by Mahmud, looking biblical as he spread the seed by hand. Then, below the lawn, the 'natural' garden, still civilised by comparison with the scrub beyond, and due to be regularised by new tree planting which will make it into an olive grove. And above the house, first vehicle access alongside the house, then a parking with bays sheltered by trees, all organised in parallel to face the view.

To emphasise the views along the length, the salon has a fireplace at the west end, the swimming pool has a recess on axis (containing showers), all connected *en enfilade*; the lawn too has a fountain on axis. Everything makes sense, and then, having made it, through sheer simplicity retreats into the background and disappears. Leaving you to pure enjoyment.

Philosophically, there is a particular enjoyment through the use of regular forms, which appeal to the intellect, due to be softened by inhabitation and by nature. This is a good use of nature, but it is also good to acknowledge that the mind is part of nature.

London, January 2004, published March 2005.

During one of those walks at Christmas C wonders aloud if she should not think of buying Martin's flat in Aix.

RM gives seminar to group at Cambridge University: *Dialectical Ambiguity in Rowe's Mannerism, 4 March.*

We decide to buy Martin's flat in Aix, 2 April.

We spend a week in the Aix apartment; staying at first with Martin, buy furniture at IKEA. It's like living all over again as students, Easter 04.

We go to a Vorticist Exhibition at the Estorick Gallery, get catalogue, 17 April.

B attends short symposium at AA on Japanese architecture, chats with Arata Isozaki, whom we last met in Paris, looking at the Pompidou Centre, when he said: "We were all doing that then!", 5 May.

RM and CS guests of Spencer and Lucy at party in Design Museum Blueprint Café, 6 June.

RM and Celia to dinner with Hogarths, meet guest Andy Watson, and we start talking about war experiences. During the handover of India, in the summer of 1947 when he was an Acting Captain, Andy was a General, 5 June.

At that time RM was commanding a platoon of Madrasis, and was based at Sialkot.

But Andy Watson was *born* in Sialkot, double putdown!

RM & Celia visit exhibition of Hopper at the Tate Modern: rather bad painter, but marvellous artist, 8 June.

The TLS ask for a review of Bernard Tschumi's book *Index Architecture.*

INDEX ARCHITECTURE
REVIEW FOR *TLS*
Edited by Bernard Tschumi and Matthew Berman, MIT 2003

This book is a presentation of the School of Architecture at Columbia University, in New York. In its red-and-yellow cover it looks like a car manual, and it reads rather like one. It has adopted the guise of a technical manual in order the better to avoid any expectation of up-market rhetoric. It follows a similar strategy to Adrian Forty's book *Words and Buildings: a vocabulary of modern architecture*, where the words that crop up so often in architectural discourse are listed alphabetically, and thereby shaken out of their too-familiar associations. Here too we have an alphabetical list, and the resulting shake-up is such that it becomes almost impossible to read the book for its narrative. The narrative has to be painfully teased out from the information undoubtedly supplied. The word list is accidental in its impact, it reflects the many discussions that have taken place in the teaching studios, the more-or-less cultivated concepts of the teaching faculty rather than any consistent vocabulary of public architecture. The book demands that you use it as a manual, and impose your own method.

It makes more sense to follow the thought of the individual teachers. Bernard Tschumi, for instance, the Dean of the School, offers an introduction and an explanation. "The aim of the school is to become a creative epicentre, a place to which practitioners can look to see where architecture is going, as opposed to a school following meekly in the footsteps of the practitioners." The younger faculty are encouraged to use their teaching studios as experimental workshops, and their students as patrols across dangerous frontiers. The school should take advantage of its situation in the heart of the city, which thereby becomes its model, the big city, where multiplicity and difference foster complexity and invention. It is clear that the other model influencing this operation is the idea of the avant-garde as inventor of the future.

This is a model that Tschumi himself has followed with success. He appears in the alphabetical sequence, and his sayings are always dynamic and serious. "You must generate the question and see where it takes you, rather than taking the answer as a starting point." He himself started with a sort of theory (*The Manhattan Transcripts*, 1981), and today he constructs deconstructed buildings that stand up and that also work. "You have to make sure that architecture is not only about concepts but also about their materialization." One of his faculty, Stan Allen, has now become Dean of Architecture at Princeton University, and already has a growing practice. Most of the faculty are engaged in a similar path, but still have to work at their theory. There is no doubt that Tschumi's success has given the school a dynamic. In addition, it has a mature and equally successful architect in the person of Steven Holl, whose work, mainly in Europe, has blended practicality and a radical look.

And the school has diversity. Some members of faculty have praised fashion as a means of exploring themes that are condemned to change. Greg Lynn: "I am interested in the ability of architecture to think through changeability as a conceptual design provocation rather than as an obstacle to timelessness and good taste.". On the same page (p. 286) we have Victoria Meyers: "I met with a client recently who said: 'It seems what you are really interested in is to create things that are timeless, undatable.' I responded, 'You are absolutely correct.' The trendiness that flies through architecture can be very datable."

The predominant trend at Columbia is the use of computer graphics, not so much to simulate conventional designs, as to generate unexpected patterns. The result is that many of the visual results are enigmatic, could only be understood by passing through the event of the public criticism, a recognised tradition in architectural schools. After the work goes on display, a great deal is lost. It must also be said that the theory that everyone respects here is not the theory of science, capable of accurate prediction, but art theory, which sometimes predicts, but more often merely records a trend. Ever since Picabia, the machine has functioned as a producer of enigmas, and this applies to most of the Columbia production. Here we are glad to note that some of the quotations ascribed to Kenneth Frampton, the Ware Professor in the school, might be taken as a direct criticism of the Columbia position. "Architects should be encouraged to discriminate between science-fiction maximisation of high technology as an end in itself and the deployment of an appropriate technology as a means to a liberative and poetic end."

London, April 2004, published 19 December 2003.

RM admitted to Royal Free for eye operation to clear left tear duct; surgeon Mr Henderson, 24 June.

Operation is all right, but not as smooth as right eye last year; enormous black eye.

RM, in dark glasses, plays piano for Peter Murray in Farmiloe Building, part of Architecture Biennale, 26 June.

Young American girl is eager listener, asks for requests: "But you're too young for this stuff!" Answer: "My mum plays it all the time." Which confirms that what RM is playing is period music; from 1937, the onset of swing.

B to TLS summer party, at the Polish Hearth Club, 55 Exhibition Road; meets Alix MacSweeney.

B and C, as RSA Fellows, accept invitation to Garden Party at Buck House and walk around lake, 8 July.

The palace itself is a museum, at least the public rooms, one can understand why Diana hated it.

Death of Jacques Derrida, with whom we had dinner at Mary Ann Caws, New York, 30 September 1987, October.

Eleanor Scott accepted into residential home at St Neots; Julian drives her there and C prepares room, 1 November.

We have the room ready, with her familiar furniture, before she arrives.

B and C to Aix for two weeks, start by driving to La Gaffe for Christmas with Julian and Teresa, 24 December.

Earthquake near Banda Aceh, Sumatra causes massive tsunami, drowning maybe 250,000, 26 December.

David and Sue Holladay, on holiday in Sri Lanka, are caught in the tsunami, but escape. They got up to higher ground; when they got back to their hotel, it was the only building left standing.

New Year's Eve we visit Rick & David for lunch, on the terrace, in the warm sun, admire garden, 31 December.

2005

We are invited to Robert's housewarming at Kennington Park Road: C prepares drawing as present, 21 January.

Peter Davey asks B to do an obituary on Philip Johnson. He supplies it immediately, 9 February.

OBITUARY OF PHILIP JOHNSON
FOR *THE ARCHITECTURAL REVIEW*

A momentous event, the death of Philip Johnson: for now Peter Eisenman can take over. He always said that so long as Philip lived, the competition to succeed him would be premature, and he himself could only be number two (though his own career doesn't seem to have held back, with thousand of pilgrims already on their way to Santiago de Compostela). But it was certainly assumed by the New York architects that Philip was number one, in other words, had led modern architecture throughout his career.

His website points to two revolutions that he fomented: first in 1938, when he published with Henry-Russell Hitchcock *The International Style*, which put him squarely behind the new functionalism; second in 1978, when he designed the AT&T Headquarters in Manhattan, which appeared to put postmodernism into action as the style for the corporations. In both cases, it was a question of style, and this aspect in itself has been enough to identify Philip Johnson as above all, a stylist, more concerned with how than what. "It's not what ya do, it's the way at ya do it", as Count Basie put it. Not a question for Basie, because he was working in his preferred style—swing, shortly to give way before bebop. It's certainly not easy for a jazz pianist famous for swing to turn over to bebop. It's an interesting parallel, because jazz came in at the same time as the Modern style in architecture, and both have continued, but with convolutions and changes of style, up to the present time. And both face the same problem: is there a future?

The orthodox view of modern architecture still conforms to Johnson's earlier point of view. The International Style was modern because it followed necessity, and necessity was defined through advances in technology. There is no end in sight to the advances that we may expect from technology, so we will happily go wherever it leads. There is just one difficulty, for it is advances in technology, in the computerisation of technical drawings, that have permitted Frank Gehry to build Bilbao, which looks more like art than technology. It uses chance to create interest, as a lot of modern art does; as the deconstructive style within architecture does. Philip himself demonstrated that he was equal to the deconstructive challenge, first with the Deconstruction show at MOMA in 1988, and then in subsequent works of his own. He treated deconstruction as merely a change in style, which is to refuse it its apocalyptic status.

Was Johnson right? Those who like technology in its rationalist guise will be uneasy, for it will open the way to an unknown future. By treating architecture as a question of style, and by demonstrating that he could change his style with the times, Johnson undermined the meaning of style. This is not exactly the same thing as undermining architecture, which presumably can survive changes in style. It does raise a fundamental question as to how appearance relates to reality, how form relates to content. It exposes a certain intolerant view within architecture, that views the abandonment of a style as akin to treachery. And it raises the question as to whether architecture is right to follow technology, rather that defining a place for technology within culture as a whole.

Whatever we may think about Johnson as a traitor to architecture, there is no doubt that he has been in the thick of the architectural debate for all his working life. We have to admire his intellectual skills, perhaps more that his artistic ones. His pre-eminence was demonstrated when he became the first winner of the Pritzker Prize in 1979, only a year after he had been awarded the AIA's Gold Medal. For most of his later life he maintained a continual debate by hosting a series of dinners at the Century Club, and almost all of America's senior architects have been educated there. By them at least, he will be missed.

London, 9 February 2004, published March 2005.

To *La Clemenza di Tito* at the Colosseum, impressed by production and sets: supper at Criterion, 8 February.

B has read Dalibor Vesely's book *Architecture in the Age of Divided Representation*: superb, 10 February.

He makes the point that the Baroque era was the last when science and art shared certain ideals.

RM lectures at Bath for Taina Rikala, on *Stirling's Theory*, 15 February.

We have lunch with Robert and Fanny at transformed 134 Kennington Park Road: it's very good, 20 February.

To Sadler's Wells for Pina Bausch: *Palermo, Palermo*: wall collapses, detritus accumulates, 20 February.

B takes Pat Clifford out for lunch at Dulwich Art Gallery, 21 April.

Pat was recognisable, especially her soft voice, but very shaky in her arms, didn't remember Robin Dunn or Mary Scriven. When it came to the bill, she insisted on paying: she still thought of herself as the boss!

We go to a party for Nicolette Boileau at her friend Alan Howarth's house in Ponsonby Terrace, 22 April.

C took postcards of her heads to show Nicolette, enjoyed also by Baroness Patricia Hollis, his partner.

B and C to 33A Millington Road for final clearing of house, now to be sold. Keys passed through letterbox, 27 April.

The Pugin Magazine publishes an article written by RM on the rehabilitation of a Pugin building, May.

SCHOOL CONVERSION HOXTON SQUARE
BUSCHOW HENLEY:
REVIEW FOR *THE PUGIN MAGAZINE*

The "conversion", as we used to call it, of an old disused school into a multiple use centre has certainly put new wine into an old bottle. The new wine, quite heady stuff, has itself been put together by creative management, with the building being sold to a private developer who then cooperated with two charitable organisations engaged in retraining immigrants. This has produced an interesting mixture of functions: small office units, a restaurant and catering school, a gym specialising in the martial arts and a couple of apartments on top, the whole thing costing no more than some £1.5 million. The social impetus behind the creation of this novel programme has resulted in a lively population, susceptible to the freshness of the initiative and appreciative of the good work of the architects in making the most of a tough but amiable building.

And the building itself comes through as welcoming the new life.

It was designed in the later 1860s (Pevsner dates it from 1870) by Edward Welby Pugin, eldest son of the inventor of Gothic Revival architecture. It is an early example of the School Board architecture, which was to reach its apogee in the Queen Anne style of the 1890s. It doesn't have any of that exuberance, but betrays its dependence on limited funding (the Catholics were always penalised for not being the established church), and comes over as pretty bare utilitarian architecture, but with a certain authority arising from its very truth-to-function. Hoxton Square separates into two bays, divided down the centre line by a single buttress, surmounted by a crucifix attached to a modest gable, itself surmounted by a smaller crucifix. That was all it had to establish its allegiance. One bay corresponds to the classroom wing that reaches back behind, the other to the school playground.

That lone buttress speaks for the Gothic in the system, and relates it to the religious zeal that underlay it, and that is more apparent in the adjoining church of St Monica's, also designed by Edward Pugin, a little earlier. There is still a surprise in the height of the school relative to the nave of this modest church, which it almost overshadows. But Edward, in spite of his duties to his father's fame, knew how to cut his cloth to fit the realities of the day. He is credited with the reconciliation of the Gothic Revival style, replete with rood screens and religious mystery, with the then current protestant demand for the altar to be visible from all points of the nave, and St Monica's exhibits this realism.

The first step for the architects was to ensure full use of the high classrooms: these are effectively two-storey spaces, and virtually all of them have been expanded through the addition of a mezzanine floor, kept back from intruding on the windows, but still providing useful additional floor space, perfectly suitable for desks and computer stations. With their simple balustrades of white-painted boarding they are unpretentious and intimate.

The next step is to enclose the playground. The boundary wall is rebuilt in cavity construction and steel beams rest on the inner leaf. A regular rear wall of ventilators allows a throughput of fresh air in summer without disturbing the privacy of the gym. A series of openable roof lights admits more air, and sun, and a small courtyard contains a garden, and provides an outlook. The garden is planted with ferns, its vivid greenness comes from the *Soleirolia soleirolii*, which covers the ground and goes far beyond the greenness of grass, and isn't intended for walking on. Its use here shows a thoughtfulness that goes far beyond native intelligence and begins to suggest devilish ingenuity.

Devilish ingenuity certainly comes through in the way the public circulation has been managed without gutting the structure of the building. The space occupied above by the escape stairs is used at ground level as a vestibule, communicating to a lobby which has a large window on to the new garden. The large panes of glass have a green colour, which adds to the vividness of the garden, and this is further accentuated by the use of red lighting, leading to the lift, which has doors on front and back, making it clever on the upper levels.

More ingenuity has been employed to include the two apartments. One enjoys the whole Hoxton Square frontage on the top floor and is double-storey in height; the other has been contrived on the roof, but has its bathroom with its entrance lobby, half a storey down. The upper flat has a spacious roof terrace, which ensures that its windows are set well back from the frontage and do not obtrude on the view of the building from the square.

The new roof over the upper flat, like the new roof over the ground floor gym, has been treated as a fifth facade, clad in black-stained timber boards and enlivened by an array of roof lights. The view down of the flat roof and into the courtyard garden takes on intermittently some of the qualities of a vertical wall, and this introduces a somewhat surreal note into the architecture. In combination with the clever planning of the access system and the clever grouping of the service elements, we have reached a level of sophistication far removed from the simple belief that sustained the original design.

Finally, the only material change to the appearance of the building is the enlargement of the ground floor windows, which become French doors opening the restaurant to its terrace in the sun. It's a compliment to the architects to say that this non-board school feature brings the building into the modern age and makes it an effective part of trendy Hoxton, on a par with the many cafes and wine bars that line the western side of the square. Yet the overall appearance of the building retains its integrity, and it can still be enjoyed as an example of Gothic Revival architecture. The sculpted lettering that used to distinguish the boy's entrance from the girl's entrance is still in place, and acts as a kind of guarantee of the genuineness of the building, and even manages to suggest its approval of its new life.

London, November 2003, published May 2005.

RM to meeting with Rick Mather, is commissioned to write a book, with Black Dog Publishing, 3 June.

Within 24 hours, London wins the 2012 Olympics designation and is hit by four bombs 7/8 July.

RM meets Bob Gutman for lunch at Artegiano's, he tells me that Aaron Lemonick, Dean of the Faculty, died, July.

We get a message of sympathy for the terrorist bombings from the Girardons in Aix, 9 July.

In Aix again, we attend John Miller's 75th birthday at his new house near Evenos. Swimpool is superb, 20 August.

The laburnum tree by our front door has been slowly leaning towards the house: we have it cut down, 8 September.

C to Scotland to stay with Charles, meets Louisa Lane Fox; C is asked to do a head of the gardener.

We attend the final installation of JS memorial plaque at Spitalfields; a small family party, 6 October.

And his ashes buried in a square hole outside the church under a stone slab incised with JS.

B is invited to RIBA to hear second annual Jencks lecture, this time given by Peter Eisenman.

With great candour, P tells of talk with his client, looking down at the immense space of Compostela.

Client: "But what is this space for?" P: "I had an inspiration. I told him 'It's for the air-conditioning'."

Eleanor has settled into her home, walks about a lot, reads *The Times*, but doesn't talk to others, 1 December.

Margaret Maxwell dies at 4.30 am in Swindon hospital, following a further stroke: cremation, Friday 2 November.

Margaret's cremation: a "service" without cleric, RM recites Auden *all the rest is silence, on the other side of the wall. And the silence ripeness, and the ripeness all*, 11 November.

We give Sunday lunch to Michael Sandle, AHC and Duncan McCorquodale, Black Dog publisher; Michael brings Penny Govett, Duncan brings Kate Trant, Madeline Vriesendorp brings Tony Fretton:

RM virtually had to kick them out when it got to 5 pm, the conversation was so good, 13 November.

RM submits brief review of Robert McCarter's *Louis Kahn* for *TLS*, e-mailed off, 10 December.

LOUIS I KAHN
BRIEF REVIEW FOR *TLS*
Robert McCarter, Phaidon, 2005

This book is a labour of love, it is steeped in reverence for a great man, no note of criticism is allowed. It is also a conscientious review of the life and work of an amazing person, someone who formed his ideas slowly in the depth of his being, and followed those ideas where they led with complete confidence and an impressive consistency. For there is no doubt that Louis Kahn is, after Le Corbusier, the major architectural thinker of the twentieth century, respected as much by Norman Foster as by Robert Venturi.

He was, for example, revered by the Smithsons: largely due to his ideas for urban planning, published as his *Plan for Midtown Philadelphia*, 1952–1953. This not only contained a planning grid of the city outlined by arrows, indicating movement (that is, emphasising process over product), but it also contained a sketch of a civic centre surrounded by monumental cylindrical parking structures, with the atmosphere of a new Rome.

Kahn began his career as a hard-working Modernist, a specialist in public housing. He didn't open his own office until 1947, at the age of 46. His first buildings were run-of-the-mill medical centres and private houses. But in 1950 he was appointed as the architect-in-residence at the American Academy in Rome, and this visit transformed his own life and changed the course of modern architecture. He was deeply impressed by Roman remains, as much by their powers of endurance as by their surfaces. As McCarter says:

> *walking through Rome, Kahn studied its monumental buildings, stripped ages ago of their decoration, their brick relieving arches revealed, their massive brick and concrete structural walls and vaults exposed, showing how they were made.*

From now on, he designed no more in steel or aluminium, but in masonry or concrete. His struggle was to be at the same time modern and monumental. Clearly, his responses to architecture were formed by a native intelligence, not by any sort of conformity to established ideas. He wished architecture to have continuity as well as novelty. In this respect he remains at the forefront of the struggle for an architecture that will be fully a part of culture.

London, December 2005, published 24 February 2006.

RM goes to Nettles for the scattering of Margaret's ashes on hill above White Horse; lunch with Bernard, 11 December.

The ceremony would have been pitiful were it not for Melinda's Bach on the oboe: that made it dignified.

We go to Aix for a blessed respite and to Bargemon with Ed and Margot for New Year's Eve, 27 December–5 January.

We have tea with the Kriers in Claviers; the space is crowded by grand pianos, the courtyard is beautiful.

2006

C starts work on her bust of Charles Jencks' gardener, does a drawing of him as a present, 6 January.

Francis House calls C to say her mother died, after a hearty lunch, while sitting in the lounge, 12 January.

We go to Cambridge for Eleanor's funeral service in Selwyn College Chapel, v. splendid, 20 January.

The service in Selwyn was splendid, full choir, all seats full; valediction by Owen Chadwick, tea afterwards.

He said she was a wonderful teacher; she was invariably given the basket cases, and got them through.

Saying goodbye to Peter Eisenman, RM is surprised when he says: Princeton is not the same without you.

RM goes to a discussion on New Towns at Alan Baxter's office; talks by Taina Rikala, Nick Bullock, 4 April.

Joseph Rykwert's 80th birthday, at the Amadeus Centre, Shirland Road, 150 people, 29 April.

The young pianist played Fats Waller on request, RM played some too; we exchanged cards.

There were friends from across the pond: Ken, Jules, George Baird, Phyllis Lambert, Mohsen, Danny and Nina.

We go with Mary Stirling for Rowe family reunion at Castle Howard, to sprinkle Colin's ashes, 27 May.

We visit Rievaulx Abbey, the Temple Terraces of Duncombe, and York Minster, magnificent.

An invitation from The Yale Center for British Art, to take part in a Symposium next November, 27 June.

By train to Chichester, for the opening of Sandy's Pallant Gallery extension, see some de Francias, 30 June.

We visit the Jas de Bouffan, where Dominic Michaelis once lived, according to CF Rowe, 25 July.

B takes Mandy to lunch at Wolseley (haddock steaks): she will leave job with builders soon, 12 August.

We go to Screen-on-the-Hill to see Antonioni's *The Passenger*: incredibly touching and beautiful, 12 August.

B writes a review of Peter Eisenman's doctoral thesis, now published by Lars Müller.

Review of Eisenman printed in *Building Design*, with a wonderful shot of Peter wearing a straight tie, 20 September.

EISENMAN:
THE FORMAL BASIS OF MODERN ARCHITECTURE
REVIEW FOR *BUILDING DESIGN*
Dissertation 1963, facsimile, L. Müller 2006

This is Peter Eisenman's Doctoral Dissertation, submitted in August 1963 at Cambridge, where he was studying under Leslie Martin, and within the orbit of Colin Rowe as tutor. It is a luxurious edition from Lars Müller, will look good on the coffee table, but has no photographs. Instead, the text is a facsimile of the original typescript—complete with the original typos; and the illustrations are drawings and tracings made by Peter himself, with his hand-printed notes.

It resembles a trophy rather than a good read. And indeed, as a read it is a difficult enterprise, since the writing is legalistic, and the thought is continuously abstract. Nevertheless, it repays study: not only as providing a clue to Eisenman as an architect, but as recording the thought of an epoch. Its argument—that form is the basis of architecture, is surely true, but we are still chary of admitting it. Such has been the vitiating effect of the doctrine of functionalism throughout the twentieth century that it is only now that architects are becoming free to present their work as in any way artistic.

Of course, architecture has to conform to controls from which art is expected to be completely free: buildings that are used are indeed linked to an economic reality that limits their freedom. And architects who ride roughshod over their clients' needs will soon be out of work. But functionalism as a doctrine was dominated by Hannes Meyer's formula: architecture is a science, the *result* of function times economy. The *source* of architectural form was from fact, not feeling. Now we realise that form comes from the imagination, conditioned as it may be, and is organised as much by mental structures as it is by empirical facts.

Eisenman has been in possession of this truth from the beginning of his career, but he has always enjoyed mystery, and enjoyed thickening rather than clarifying the situation. With this publication, however, he begins to come clean.

So here he creates another fiction: that architectural form comes complete with grammar and syntax, and is derived from ideal forms such as the Phileban solids—sphere, square, cylinder and cone. These together create generic sources, varied between the centroidal and the linear, modified by access and approach, and capable by themselves of creating a language. He adds an integrating perception derived from gestalt psychology, but rejects any thought of a picturesque control, looking instead for logic and consistency.

He demonstrates these ideas through analysis of examples by Corb, Wright, Aalto and Terragni. These analyses are impressive. They sent me back to the originals, where I saw things I had never seen before. The ground floor plan of the Swiss Hostel, for example, has an amazing subtlety, with a use of paired columns that change their axis. Eisenman has studied his sources severely.

With Corb, Eisenman's tone is deferential, with Aalto respectful, with Terragni attentive, and with Lloyd Wright critical and even outraged (he speaks of a staircase node in the Coonley House as "agonising"). These feelings come through in spite of the controlled language, which deals in axes, vectors, distortions, dislocations, plaids that reconcile two major tendencies, pressures that are pent up or released. The most readable is on Terragni's Asilo Infantile, which comes last, by which time Peter has become adept at the use of his language and is clearly enjoying himself.

In her analysis of Eisenman's Houses, Rosalind Krauss saw the importance in his work of deliberate obfuscation through the creation of a complexity that keeps us guessing. This enables us to spend time with Eisenman, since his meaning is not obvious, and doesn't empty out after a brief survey. In this text the thought is so abstract that it could be read as obfuscation.

What is never put in the picture is the play of chance, which is a major factor in Eisenman's recent work. His method now is to manipulate a rich overlay of conflicting frameworks, that will together produce an interesting complexity. He is like a swimmer who goes far out before turning and making for the shore, using normal instincts to survive, and to make sense of the complexity he has himself initiated.

London, 5 September 2006, published 15 September 2006.

We go to dinner with Amy Meyers responsible for the proposed exhibition of JS; we are Mary's guests, 20 October.

B gives his last lecture at the AA (*Homage à Barthes*) followed by reception for 125 invited guests, 22 November.

The lecture hall had names on all the seats except the last two rows, which were filled by students.

At the reception after the lecture, RM much affected by Mary Douglas saying: "It was liberating!"

2007

B to Cambridge by train to deliver C's brochure for Attenborough to Wendy Pullan at Clare College, 24 January.

A visit to Flowers Gallery in Cork Street for an Eduardo show, C's head displayed as 'self-portrait', 6 February.

C writes to correct them, and claim authorship of the bust of Eduardo.

Clare College in touch about cost of Attenborough bust, which means he must have chosen C, 14 March.

Sandy Wilson has died, we hear it from Robert: B is to read from Bunyan at the funeral, 16 May.

"And the trumpets sounded from the other side"

To St John's Wood church for Sandy's funeral; B just about manages to get through his reading, 23 May.

Mary Douglas has died, we are invited to the funeral by her daughter Janet Farnsworth, 23 May.

To St Patrick's, Soho Square for Mary Douglas's funeral; then reception under the trees in Bedford Square, 5 May.

A tribute to Mary Douglas was read out by one of several Lele present, more moving than the funeral itself.

They were the tribe with which she did her field work. They said she was kindness itself.

To celebrate B's birthday, we go to the RA show on seascapes, followed by dinner at Wolseley's, 6 July.

There, chat is dominated by C's worry about her book, but redeemed by the sight of Paul McCartney.

RM receives e-mail inviting him to a conference on Rowe in March 2008 in Venice, responds "Yes", 3 September.

Given choice of subject, he elects to speak on *Collage City*, and Rowe's contribution to city planning.

RM travels alone to the States, asking for a wheelchair: this whizzes him to the head of the queue, 26 October.

The Stirling Exhibition is set for 2010, and Tony Vidler agreed to be curator of it. The minute that was agreed, we broke for lunch at Scoozzi's, showing us that decision was the real purpose.

RM invited to Florence by Francisco Sanin, to give *Rowe & Mannerism* for Syracuse Program, 11 November.

RM has Michael Wilford to lunch at the Athenaeum, collects package of stuff on the Peace Palace, 20 November.

The Peace Palace Library, The Hague,
Wilford Schupp Architects 2008

THE PEACE PALACE LIBRARY, THE HAGUE
WILFORD SCHUPP ARCHITECTS:
REVIEW FOR *THE ARCHITECTURAL REVIEW*

The new building accommodates a major expansion of the Peace Palace Library, along with new facilities for the Hague Academy of International Law. Both activities have been given an individual identity within a single new building comprising a triangular Reading Room, an oval Academy Hall, and a connecting volume containing foyer, offices and ancillaries. The Peace Palace was designed by Louis Cordonnier in 1913 in a fairly elaborate Flemish Gothic style. It contains the International Court of Justice and the Permanent Court of Arbitration. The connection to the Palace is made at first floor level through the reading room, which thus serves equally for the new library and what remains of the old library—the old Historic Reading Room—while under it an entrance at ground level gives access to the new building and the new auditorium, also at ground level. The entrance foyer extends upwards through three of the four storeys, and provides internal visual connections that convey an idea of the whole, and reinforce the sense of community. The upper level of the spine contains new offices for the Hague Academy of International Law and the International Court of Justice, as well as the Permanent Court of Arbitration. So this is a vital building not only for Europe, but for justice in the world.

This brief description is sufficient to show that the building is directly functional in conception, and takes its cue from primary aspects of connection and circulation.

The new building is related visually to the old by being faced with a matching brick, but this is clearly a hung facade on a frame and makes no attempt to compromise with the architectural style, while the use of a metal skin on the reading room and auditorium, along with extensive glazing, makes it clear that we are living in a new world. This sense of a new beginning is reinforced by the bright yellow pilotis, arranged in two V-s, that support the reading room, and the no-nonsense purple rendering that picks out the upper galleries in both reading room and auditorium, and defines the wall backing the registration desk. Colour is also provided from the yellow ceiling and the red wall at the west end that marks the presence of the Academy. The result is a vibrant modern building full of *joie de vivre* and the sense of an optimistic future.

There is a clear relation, not only to the old Peace Palace, but to the formal garden which surrounds it, and which the new building complements. It takes the place of a 1929 building which was judged to be not up to its future role and was demolished, and it has improved the garden in its southwest corner by providing a better termination to the north–south axis, which now finishes squarely on the auditorium. A new car access occupies the space between the old and new buildings, while the auditorium has extensive views right across the width of the garden. Service deliveries are made from a hard court that abuts the backs of houses along the south side.

What then of the expression, of the architectural language employed?

There is a combination of very precise rational planning with expressive elements that stand out for their chutzpah. The triangular reading room and the oval auditorium both employ curves, one in section, the other mainly in plan. The stainless steel skin that covers the reading room is tailored to an ideal section, as if it were made out of one piece; it is, however, composed of lozenges that can maintain the surface over quite sharp curves. Where the space of the reading room faces the foyer, the lozenges continue indoors, while the vertical face at the end is covered with flat metal, thus illustrating the shape of the section. These lozenges reappear on the solid vertical wall of the auditorium, which frames the extensive glass wall, which is supported by tapering mullions, leaning gently outward and curving back sharply at the top. The use of curves, in plan and section, seems to identify these elements as being part of an expressive modern world.

More aggressive is the use of sharp angles in the triangular plan of the reading room. The approximately 45 degree angle is received by the entrance foyer without any fuss, since it happens at the upper level where the receiving space is divided into a narrow balcony and equally narrow external terrace, but the similar thrust of the library balcony into the upper part of the reading room is emphasised by its bright purple colour; and even more is the angle which, purple as ever, appears outside on the south elevation. The same angle reappears in the half landing of the stairs up on the left of the entrance, but again is passed off without any fuss. The details continue as if unconscious of the implied danger, and sew the architecture together. Nevertheless, the nonchalance maintained by the architect in managing these sharp points is impressive.

Impressive too is the ease with which the structure has been managed internally. The frame is evident mostly as cylindrical columns, four of which support the internal edge of the reading room, as well as two groups of four that appear inside the reading room. Along the edge of the reading room gallery these are replaced with steel mullions, and along the length of the rear foyer they are replaced with cruciform steel columns. The structure in the brick walls, on both north and south sides, is contained in fairly massive brick piers, continuous with the walls above. There is no ideology about the structure as such, it takes the form it has to out of a sense of duty, without fuss.

Dealing with Michael Wilford as architect, one can't help being conscious of his debt to Jim Stirling, and look to find remnants of Stirling's mastery. Yet here, the impression I receive is, rather, how much Big Jim must have taken from Michael. This architecture is very confident, it follows through on the decisions made in the initial diagram without awkwardness, without balking, and brings the design to a triumphant conclusion. It is completely self-sufficient.

It is also very effective as functional design. Consider all the configurations of which the lecture hall is capable. It can focus equally well on the wide window wall, or along its length to the division between wall and window. It can accommodate a conference for 150 delegates and 100 observers, or allow audiovisual presentations to an audience of 320 people. Lighting levels are controlled by blinds. The large window faces north and doesn't bring heat-gain. One comes to realise that the oval plan is not only highly expressive, but is crucial to the variety of uses.

Or consider the expressive shape of the reading room. It squishes out to kiss the old building, without subservience. But internally, it is a horizontal space of considerable intimacy, with discreet lighting, which encourages concentrated work. For expressive reasons, the volume diminishes in section towards the old building, and this is managed internally by angled ceilings, and by gentle ramps on the floor, on one side, and groups of steps on the other, that work smoothly without causing trouble. At the level of use, the expressive gesture has been absorbed without trace; but it is still there.

The main thrust of the architectural expression is concentrated in the two large rooms, the rest is treated as everyday theatre, and it receives everyday banality without a problem. But the foyer as a whole is energised by the organisation of the daylighting through an array of windows, and by a variety of views both upward and downward. It does make a single shared space which works for the institution as a whole, and it seems to express a democratic ideal, appropriate for the idea of world justice.

And another thing strikes one. The red screen which seems to define the Academy is decorated. Decoration used to be anathema to modern architects. Here it happens naturally, and creates no problem. This bas-relief was designed by Irene Fortuyn: it consists of a bas-relief made of maps of all the countries of the world, rearranged randomly. At one level it is purely decorative; at another level it expresses the presence of the countries that will benefit from world justice. Not in their normal geographic hierarchy, but in a presentation where all are equal. One cannot say that world justice has been achieved. Not in Darfur, certainly. To achieve it will require time and effort, and the dedication of good men. This building looks forward to that time. Until it comes, it seems to say, one may as well be cheerful.

London, April 2008, published October 2008.

Weekend with Charles and Louisa at Portrack, 11 to 13 April. Guests include Kristin Feireiss, curator of the Aedes Gallery, visited for David Chipperfield in September 1995, very friendly.

Charles wants RM to write 1,500 words on the garden, and get it published. Paul Finch interested for AR.

On Sunday RM walked the garden alone, couldn't help being impressed, but by what? An aura? Words, maybe.

Or the way in which words coincide with the actual experience of the landscape.

Reviews of Simone de Beauvoir say she seduced girls then passed them on to Sartre; both monsters! 20 April.

RM publishes three reviews: in AR: Murray Fraser; in BD: Richard Meier and Joseph Rykwert.

THE AMERICAN INFLUENCE ON POST-WAR BRITISH ARCHITECTURE
REVIEW FOR *THE ARCHITECTURAL REVIEW*
Murray Fraser, Joe Kerr: Architecture and 'Special Relationship', Routledge 2008

I enjoyed this book: it takes a very positive view of the United States, and its influence on the United Kingdom, and is fair about the influences that this country had on the States. The authors clearly enjoy both places. There is a long bibliography, the authors have done their homework, the book is well balanced and objective, and well edited. It is a must for architectural libraries.

Of course, it is particularly enjoyable as a history of the immediate past, dealing with a period that one has oneself lived through. The only criticisms I have are fairly minor ones: my memory of Reyner Banham is that he respected Colin Rowe, as did Rowe Banham; they were each careful about the other, and were seen as the poles of a dialectic: Banham strong on empirical facts, Rowe perhaps unduly sensitive to architectural form. Rowe's influence was largely due to the importance he gave to theory, about which Banham was disdainful. I enjoyed his use of the Moulton bicycle, but also liked the way he learned to drive a car in order to thoroughly understand Los Angeles. The book has a stunning photograph of Banham riding his small cycle across the dry bed of a lake in California.

In dealing with the important influence of Llewelyn Davies, Fraser ignores the vital role played by John Weeks. He was the designer in that office, his hand is evident in the building for London Zoo and the hospital at Northwick Park, and it was he who went to the US to look for models for a planning grid premised on the car. Milton Keynes is the most successful of all the New Towns, probably because of its situation halfway between London and Birmingham.

There is plenty of fascinating detail. Did you know that Berthold Lubetkin had a statue of Lenin (a bust, perhaps?) erected in London; then quietly dismantled it and buried it under an Islington school playground?

The most successful aspect of the book is the way it deals with the Smithsons, and their search for perennial values, in the wake of Louis Kahn. Considering how their influence evaporated after the Economist Building, there is a tragic aspect to their loss of commissions, and this section of the narrative I found quite moving. Denise Scott Brown took Peter's remark "Port Grimaud is almost all right", and came up with "Main Street is almost all right", and she has been a feisty influence on Robert Venturi all through. On the other hand, the search for perennial values is still strong, as can be seen in the quiet work of David Chipperfield, Tony Fretton, Eric Parry, none of whom get a look-in. In dealing with an ongoing story, you have to draw the line somewhere.

London, June 2008, published October 2008.

THE JUDICIOUS EYE
REVIEW FOR *BUILDING DESIGN*

Joseph Rykwert: *The Judicious Eye: Architecture Against The Other Arts,*
Reaktion, 2008

Architecture was originally the mother art, which provided sites for painting and sculpture, shelter for music and performance. But in the twentieth century critics generally united under the banner of functionalism and characterised it as a sort of applied science. Sir John Summerson reluctantly seemed to accept this idea in his 1957 lecture at the RIBA, when he admitted modern architecture to be based on following the programme. So there has been a tendency to deny it the status of art, and to separate it from the arts.

This separation has increased enormously since the 1950s, and it evidently gives Joseph Rykwert pain. He writes rather of an architecture that is clearly one of the arts. The history of building over the past half century, he says, can be written as an account of the increasing privatisation of the public realm. The impact of painting and sculpture on how the man-made environment looks and feels has been weakening. Architecture has become the site for publicity, as at Piccadilly Circus or Times Square, it is becoming a mere servant to real estate development, which is squarely focussed on making money. Events like Gehry at Bilbao, or practically anything proposed for Abu Dhabi or Dubai have merely reinforced the gimmickry that Sandy Wilson bemoaned as "icon architecture".

Rykwert doesn't do much to resolve this problem, which is surely a demanding one. What he does do is to chronicle the history of architecture as a partner with the other arts, from the Adam brothers in mid-eighteenth century to the end of the twentieth century. This is a story which he tells superbly, and with gusto. It makes enjoyable reading.

I am grateful for the ease with which he puts to work his immense knowledge, the way he can move between people and events. He knows all the names, who was there and who wasn't. There is a sense in which culture is borne along on conversation, and here we seem to be on the edge of hearing those conversations, and joining in that continual buzz of excitement that goes with fresh discoveries. On the way there is plenty to surprise.

To realise, for example, that Wagner was of the left, not the right (p. 138); that Semper was on the point of emigrating to the USA when he was recalled to Paris with the possibility of a commission (p. 140); that Ford Madox Ford in Rome met Overbeck and Cornelius, members of the Nazarene group that romanticised the Middle Ages, and from that conversation was active in helping to found the Pre-Raphaelite Brotherhood in London (p. 149). That Walter Pater applied for ordination as the Bishop of London (p. 173).

The result is a narrative that moves effortlessly between larger events like the formation of a group, or the organisation of a festival, and the efforts called forth by those ideas in the lives of individuals. When Tolstoy wrote the epitaph to *War and Peace*, he was concerned with the difference between the tides of history, which seem to follow ineluctable rules, and the individuals caught up in those tides, who continue to feel free. Rykwert seems to operate in just that zone where general ideas influence the individual to new creation.

Of course, there are omissions. We are shown Wagner's Festspielhaus in Bayreuth, and struck by the similarity in its volumes to Garnier's Paris Opera, but nothing is said about the Paris Opera. Nothing is said about Berlage's Holland House in London, which combines fine sculpture with a rational facade. No mention is made of Hoffmann's Palais Stoclet, where the conversation, the women's dresses and the men's cigars were all seen as the completion of the artistic whole, although we might think them mere indulgence. Nothing is said about Hinton's book about the *Fourth Dimension*, or about Dora Henderson's full discussion of it.

In fact, the search for contiguity between the arts, as with colours and music, is chronicled in a tolerant way without much comment on the zaniness of much of it. A great deal of the excitement generated by one art upon another seems in retrospect to be merely silly. And the search for the *Gesamtkunstwerk* means that performance art becomes sort of privileged.

The fact is that politics is the real motivation behind the use of public spaces in the city and, while many demonstrations are stage-managed, others are genuine outpourings of public anxiety. Oxford Street is all about consumption, but Trafalgar Square is sometimes serious. And of course, museums have displaced churches as the preferred places where people go to develop their individual souls. So we are left with the initial problem. Is there a future for public architecture?

London, July 2008, published 11 July 2008.

RICHARD MEIER: COMPLETE WORKS
REVIEW FOR *BUILDING DESIGN*
Richard Meier & Partners: Complete Works, Taschen, 2008

Alberto Campo Baeza, an architect whom I greatly respect, has written a very poetic introduction to this book, in which he casts Richard Meier as a latter-day Ulysses, lashed to the mainmast of Architecture and resisting the siren seductions of money, fame and power. He proposes his eventual return to Ithaca, to a waiting Penelope, who, it seems, is also Architecture. Ithaca, New York, is real, Cornell University there is Meier's *Alma Mater*, and no doubt he does go back there from time to time as a renowned alumnus, or to undertake more design. The rest is poetic license.

But it is true that, as Baeza says, in spite of the work having won every prize going, there is a curious silence among critics about the achievement of this work. This massive volume, too heavy to read in bed (it needs to be firmly placed on a reading table) is the answer to that silence.

It is a monumental volume, carried out with the same consistency that attaches to Meier's architecture. Each project is treated in the same way, with an introductory two page spread, followed by site plan and ample plan drawings, individual views and finally, a sunset or night view. The photography is superb. Skies are usually blue, the white walls gleam, it is clearly the best of all possible worlds. The consistency gives a sense of completeness. And that, maybe, is part of the problem. This consistency makes it look easy, too easy to require struggle, or to call forth unexpected results. When you employ Richard Meier as an architect, you have a pretty good idea of what it is that you will get. His work is trademarked by its consistent style.

Yet it is also true that the scope of his work is enormous. The book lists some 240 jobs that the office has handled over the years, but only fifty of these are illustrated, presumably the 50 best. So it is highly selective. Yet one suspects that the 190 left out would be sufficient in themselves to establish a whole career in architectural design. The missing works arouse one's curiosity, just as one would like to see the sides of the illustrated works not shown, like the rear ends of the twin towers at Perry Street, or the curved corners at the rear of the Douglas House.

Meier has been famous ever since he was introduced as one of the New York Five, in Arthur Drexler's exhibition at MOMA in 1969, and subsequently in the book *Five Architects* of 1972. All five of them were marked by the influence of Le Corbusier. Hejduk died, Graves went PoMo, Gwathmey vernacular, Eisenman deconstructivist, only Meier has stayed clearly within the Corbu influence, and has evolved it slowly into a manner that is utterly personal while remaining utterly modern. But this can be put in another way. In the Smith House of 1967 and still more, in the Douglas House of 1973, Meier has already invented features that will become established with the passage of time as typically his.

What he seems to do is to play with these features as if they were the words of a language, creating an amazing variety out of elements that themselves remain virtually unchanged, which is exactly what language is capable of. The white walls are often composed of porcelain enamelled panels, which give the buildings a purity that makes them almost abstract in their ideality. But the whiteness also reflects light to take on the completeness of sculptural form.

Although most of Meier's work is deliberately rectangular in character, he does make use of curves, usually in plan, sometimes in elevation, as a means of enlivening the composition. The Stadthaus at Ulm is an example of a systematic use of the circle in plan. The Getty Center, of 1984–1997, uses curves to emphasise focal points in a huge layout which, although apparently picturesque, is governed by a strict geometry in its setting out.

There can be no question about Meier's originality. But he is also very knowledgeable about precedent. Philip Johnson, in his postscript to *Five Architects*, wrote: "Meier knows his history best of the five, studies it most, learns from it most." His work is full of references to buildings of modern architecture.

His consistency of style does allow him to play with architecture as we play with words. But his design (in collaboration with Eisenman, Gwathmey and Holl) for the competition entry for the World Trade Center Memorial Square uses a gridded motif in elevation to make a stunning image. His Jubilee Church, in Rome, uses curves both in plan and elevation to make a beautiful space. His protective structure for the Ara Pacis is the height of discretion. Within the regularity of his vocabulary his compositions have an amazing variety. His architecture has matured into a sophisticated ability to follow the programme rather than distort it. And with skyscrapers now twisting themselves into a variety of shapes in order to project their freedom as art, this reticence is something for which we can be grateful.

London, June 2008, published 27 June 2008.

RM and CS go to the Wallace Collection for the opening of a Princeton University Conference, 20 to 21 June.

On the second day Oppenheimer was good on climate change; Shirley Tilghman, the President, made a very Princeton speech.

Celia writes a piece for *AA Files*, around the picture of Léon and Ken in the book, very good, 23 June.

RM participates in Histories and Theories Dissertations discussion (David Dunster, Wendy Pullan), 26 June.

Instead of joining them all for dinner, RM goes to TLS summer party, held this year in 40 Brunswick Square.

RM has lunch at Athenaeum hosted by Charles Jencks, with Zaha, Terry Farrell and Dean Robert Stern, 4 July.

After Last Supper now First Dinner with John and Su in their new Clerkenwell flat: with Ken & Sylvia.

To Venice for four days, RM speaks on *Collage City and Rowe's urbanism*, with slides, 5 to 9 March.

Also met: P Eisenman, Georges Tessyot, Alessandra Ponte, Francesco Dal Co.

To Sally and Richard for the weekend at Southwell; amazed at Southwell Minster; Norman nave, 16 to 18 May.

At a great concert in Wigmore Hall, we meet the Rykwerts, the Jones, Jeremy Dixon and Julia, 13 June.

And Alan Bowness and his sister-in-law, who once told him in 3 Mall Studios: "I lived in this room till I was 5."

Exciting to visit Thoresby Park again (the Villa Caldogno) and to be taken round by Hugh Matheson, 17 May.

RM meets Alan Berman (Bartlett student in Diploma 1975) who is writing a book about Stirling, 7 August.

RM to write 5,000 word scene-setting essay, chapter 1 in book, followed by Alan's description of the red brick series.

C has a book *Sorry No Gas* from Phyllis Lambert, with a friendly note of congratulation on her book, 8 September.

RM writes the piece he promised to do for Charles Jencks: Paul Finch interested for AR.

The Garden of Cosmic Speculation
Portrack, Charles Jencks

THE GARDEN OF COSMIC SPECULATION
REVIEW FOR *ARCHITECTURAL REVIEW*

I was privileged to be a weekend guest at Portrack recently, and took the opportunity of wandering the garden on my own, having already heard Charles' explanation for everything. Strangely, the power of words became more telling when I couldn't hear Charles' voice. There are still words, on slabs of stone, mostly, or on banners hung from trees. The landscape combines with these words in a magic way. It puts me in mind of Thomas Love Peacock's descriptions of landscape, as in *Headlong Hall*:

> *... but it was reserved for the exclusive genius of the present times to invent the noble art of picturesque gardening, which has given, as it were, a new tint to the complexion of nature, and a new outline, to the physiognomy of the universe.*

The English invention of the picturesque garden can be seen as a major contribution to world culture: it deploys the prime English quality of good form in the prime English style, which is that it should be invisible, and never referred to in words. Artifice there is in abundance, but it looks as if this is nature's own artifice. It *looks* natural.

Now Charles Jencks, inspired by his former partner Maggie Keswick, has gone further. He manipulates the landscape, glorying in the artifice, digging out ponds and piling up the material to form mounds. It is artifice, indeed, but the grass that grows on the mounds is real. And, when it rains, or gets frosty, or snows, it remains "the place beneath", and is re-integrated into the natural landscape. So, more clearly than before, through vivid contrasts and juxtapositions, landscape, while remaining in one sense inert, becomes in another sense a fluid material, a means even of expressing ideas.

And these ideas, sparked by a few words, are about man's place in nature, and so man's place in the cosmos. We are so used to thinking of landscape as natural, that we tend to extend the nature we know indefinitely, while the landscape that is so familiar to us is really just the girl next door. When we consider that the biosphere, the habitable part of the world, is nothing but a thin shell, a mile or so thick, approximating to the surface of the earth, this nature becomes tiny. In cosmological terms, in relation to the cosmos, it is minute. Yet the cosmos is also natural, it consists, as far as we know, of the same material, the same elements, that we learned at school.

But it is also mysterious. We cannot as yet account for the presumed weight of the universe, and to explain what we know we have had to hypothesise an invisible *dark matter*, only fathomed through its effect on light. And that alone is not enough to account for the theoretical weight of the universe, we have had to presume the existence of another element, which we call *dark energy*, for which no physical evidence exists. In a further complication, the more we know about the forces inside the atom, the more mysterious matter becomes. There is a surprising number of subatomic particles, most of them short-lived, and again it is difficult to account for the weight of things; this is why so much is riding on the so-called Higgs boson, whose existence has been hypothesised, and whose discovery would allow us to derive the weight of matter more satisfactorily, by completing the standard model of the atom, linking weight (gravity) to the three other forces inside the atom (Electromagnetism, the Weak Force, the Strong Force).

It is this wider framing of nature that Charles Jencks wishes to bring to our attention; and where better to do this than in the heart of the countryside, or rather, of a garden, where nature dominates but at the same time can be subverted. So we arrive at the *Garden of Cosmic Speculation*, the title of Charles Jencks' book, the essence of which will be to discover "a new grammar of landscape design to bring out the basic elements of nature that recent science has found to underlie the cosmos." At the origin of the design is a reflection of the basic character of the Scottish lowlands—low hills grazed by animals—which led to a geometry of curves. But the first major task was to drain a swamp, and this led to a discovery of the power of the machine, and to the principal of piling up the excavated material to form mounds, and to the possibility of combining the ups and downs by the use of spirals and writhing forms, and so they were off (Maggie and Charles) on a path that was to have many convolutions.

They started with the water, now enlarged to become a small lake, and by building a promontory into it created two dragons—a Land Dragon, and a Water Dragon. So metaphor was to engulf the whole programme. A major idea of life as the enjoyment of the senses became a theme that would give rise to the Garden of Common Sense (the

Kitchen Garden), the Garden of the Six Senses, the tennis court as the Sense of Fair Play, the Wood where the crows quarrelled almost every evening as Taking Leave of Your Senses, and The Nonsense.

The Nonsense was a construction: a mock-up of part of James Stirling's Neue Staatsgalerie in Stuttgart, rescued from oblivion and put to use as a parable of No Sense, with the addition of words by Baudelaire ("*La Nature est un temple, ou de vivants piliers/ laissent parfois sortir de confuses paroles*")—the first of many episodes where words are seeded into the visitor's experience of the landscape. The book contains some memorable shots of The Nonsense being visited by Léon Krier, and later by Stirling and Paolozzi, making one regret that their conversation has been lost.

> *Words, letters, signs, symbols should reverberate throughout a landscape, an idea common to Chinese gardens and poet-gardeners such as Ian Hamilton Finlay.*

So says Jencks (p. 44), and there can be no doubt that Hamilton Finlay has provided a model for Portrack. In his garden at Little Sparta a cottage is ennobled with four corinthian pilasters and the words: "To Apollo—His Music, His Missiles, His Muses." The Chinese influence is also obvious in the choice of bright red as the colour for many inserts into the landscape, as with the Jumping Bridge (p. 140) or the columns in Quark Walk.

Quark Walk is my own favourite episode. It's been named partly for its intrinsic sound, as is obvious from there being no equivalent Lepton Walk (Quarks and Leptons are part of the initial division of subatomic particles, more or less equal and opposite, but Lepton Walk sounds like a suburb of Edinburgh). Quark Walk leads from Crow Wood, which contains The Nonsense) to the Jumping Bridge and Slug Lakes, and it follows the path of a stream (a "burn", in this neck of the woods). Wooden stumps painted bright red form quasi-temples where the equations of interatomic maths are written. The path is complicated by the intervention of a chain link fence (a defense against the rabbits), which gives it some of the obstinacy of an obstacle course. In the tension of not falling into the stream, reading the words "Higgs boson" can strike terror into the heart.

The garden's most striking episode must be the combination of Slug Lakes and the associated mounds—Snake Mound and Snail Mound. It is quite an experience to walk between the lakes on a grass-covered embankment, and to feel simultaneously one's performance as player in a Landscape Folly, and one's experience as a child of nature. It is this image which has reappeared in Jencks' design for the land behind the Gallery of Modern Art in Edinburgh, and which has reappeared again in his proposal for Portello Park in Milan.

But the most disturbing episode must be the construction called "Cascading Universe", which combines a mound, a lake and a garden of forking paths, all constructed as a set of joining steps, leading up to a building, indubitably modern in style. If you keep your head, you are safe enough, but the ascent does remind one rather of those Mexican pyramids where you simply have to keep your head. (See the aerial photograph on pp. 242–243.) Here also there is a pond, but it is more constrained by the land forms containing it, and elaborated by knife-like metal blades, and it ends up as a brooding presence. Moreover, it is all deeply symbolic of the universe, its age measured in units of time going from fractions of a second to billions of years. There are stone fragments weirdly reminiscent of parts of the body, and water channels that look like the world is splitting up. I escaped from this set piece with a sense of relief.

More reassuring is the part of the garden that adjoins the rail track from Dumfries to Glasgow, where trains pass at frequent intervals. Charles was able to negotiate with the Rail Company to redesign their bridge over the River Nith, to conserve part of the abandoned bridge as a cantilever, and to help construct a series of small mounds in a row, as if they were wagons pulled by a locomotive, and even to put in place a real locomotive at their head. With all the steelwork painted the red of the Jumping Bridge, it falls into the language of the garden, and constitutes *The Garden of Scottish Worthies*, a record of the Enlightenment. The small mounds carry the signs of Enlightenment thinkers pulled by the 'train of progress', while the row of poplar trees holds red aluminium signs with important dates and names, events, massacres, that punctuated Scottish history, a story that Charles calls "The Bloodline". It becomes the Low Road ("You take the Low Road, I'll take the High Road, I'll be in Scotland afore you".) The events of the history of a few hundred years are less disturbing, if more real, than the billions of years covered in the Cascading Universe, and the result is a sense of relaxation, in spite of the bloodiness and strife actually commemorated.

I have said nothing about many other episodes: the metal models of atoms and double helixes that adorn the Garden of the Six Senses and DNA, the Black Hole Terrace, the Symmetry Break Terrace, the Linear Paradise Garden, the Willow Twist, where moss first refused to grow, then grew in abundance. There is something genuinely poetic about the words used in these names.

The story of the garden becomes a kind of record of family history, as well as a creation of the mind. Perhaps the most enjoyable feature for the ordinary visitor is the many gates designed to celebrate some aspect of science: these are all strangely beautiful. And the book is also something, well designed and laid out, with wonderful pictures. The picture on p. 26 has Maggie flanked by a younger Frank Gehry and an even younger Michael Graves, enough in itself to make the book a compulsive buy.

London, October 2008, published November 2008.

To USA for rededication of Paul Rudolph Hall at Yale; British Airways, met by limo at JFK, 7 November.

Put up at the Colony Inn (used in old times) now known as the Study at Yale, 1157 Chapel Street.

Meet lots of old friends: Charles Gwathmey, Stephen Harris, Tom Beeby, Deborah Berke, Koetter and Kim, Judy DiMaio, Peggy Deamer, Kurt Forster, George Baird, Vince Scully, Joel Sanders, Alex Tzonis, Peter Eisenman, Paul Goldberger, Norman Foster, the Petersons, Richard and Ruth Rogers.

RM Impressed by wonderful photo of Rudolph chatting to a starry-eyed Bob Stern, between them a girl identified as MJ Long.

Trip to Princeton, 10 November. It was good to see Princeton again, once part of everyday life.

RM verified that PJ's Pancake house was still operating, very noisily, so we had quiet coffee at the Bread Shop.

Saw a part of Nassau Street, saw Lahiere's, Woolworth's, the bookshop, now enlarged, the Annexe, all once so familiar. And visited Michael Graves for a long chat, interrupting his painting of a large panel, very friendly.

RM and C to AA for discussion on Corb's visit in 1947, well chaired by Joseph Rykwert, 28 November.

Speakers included Paffard Keatinge-Clay (no memories on either side) and Kenneth Frampton.

2009

We go to Cornwall for Su's 70th birthday; taxis at train, to Tresanton Hotel, 23–24 January. Lunch on beach below hotel, suckling pig, mulled wine, very festive, R Rogers in bare feet. Eating minestrone while the tide laps round your feet is quite a sensation; chat with John Miller. Later, dancing, sporadic; at interval, RM on keyboard has enthusiastic audience, including Richard and Ruth.

At AA symposium on *Palladio* RM meets Ziba Rastegar married to Rupert von Preussen, 14 March.

In answer to my question, Howard Burns reveals that the blank panel at Casa Cogollo was backed by a fireplace.

And was meant to receive a painting, as at the Zuccheri Casino; so much for Palladio as a Mannerist!

Although he did make extensive use of the giant order as put forward by Michelangelo.

We attend lectures by Robert Venturi and Denise Scott Brown at AA, and the dinner afterwards, 30 April.

RM buys a copy of her book *Having Words*, and gets her to sign it; both of them very friendly.

To Neave Brown's 80th party at Lauderdale House, Highgate; good food, Gordon Benson gave best speech, 16 May.

Pina Bausch has died, 30 June.

Supper followed by *Phèdre* at the National Theatre, car parked underneath; no interval, 22 August.

It was fascinating; but we were both disappointed with Helen Mirren, all action, she seemed to lack gravitas.

Rereading the original text, one realises how important was the regular beat of Racine's versification:

Ce n'est plus une ardeur dans mes veines cachée, c'est Vénus tout entière à sa proie attachée

Good chat with Ken, he pointed out that in the 60s I talked both to the Rowe faction and the Banham one.

RM has lunch at Athenaeum with Michael Wilford, who wants a piece on Melsungen, 22 January.

MICHAEL WILFORD AT MELSUNGEN
REVIEW FOR *ARCHITECTURE TODAY*

I last visited Melsungen in May 1992, with James Stirling, for the inauguration of his building for Georg Braun, which he designed together with his partner Michael Wilford and the German Walter Nägeli; that was nearly eighteen years ago. It is a plant that produces plastic products for medical science. It is rather a series of buildings, combining to form a sort of industrial campus, and has already been added to since then; and today it has been transformed by a crucial addition designed by Michael Wilford and his partner Manuel Schupp.

Modern architecture, when it first appeared in the 20s, was dedicated to the idea of serving function, and one important aspect of that was the recognition, eventually, that serving function means a capability of adaptation to change. Richard Rogers expressed this attitude succinctly:

> *The history of architecture should be seen as a history of social and technical invention and not of styles and forms. It is those periods when change quickens and turning points are reached, when innovation is more important than consolidation and the perfecting of style, that interest me most. I prefer Brunelleschi to Michelangelo....*[1]

I myself have always preferred Michelangelo to Brunelleschi, precisely because he comes later, and takes account of the play of form in the equation, which means that he knowingly uses rhetoric to put his art over to the public. An understanding of the way rhetoric works to communicate ideas is essential to the understanding of meaning in art and architecture, and part of that is the understanding of the uncertainty implicit in all forms of expression, even in the direct accommodation of newness, so admired by Richard Rogers.

Adding to a building 18 years after its inception must be considered as coming later, and no doubt this explains why Michael Wilford has belatedly seized the opportunity to add a main entrance portico to an already functioning building.

It was a building complex that in its initial layout already anticipated change, so the masterplan incorporated within its layout spaces that could be filled in later. The production building, for example, was expected to grow, and in the initial phase space was allowed for this at both ends of a long shed. After 18 years the production has increased by some 50 per cent, and this is taken care of by elongating the end nearest to the public approach, and terminating it by a high roof overhang, which creates a vivid portico.

The vast majority of visitors are interested in viewing the process of production, and this was already the case from the building's inception. In the original layout, the staff welcoming visitors were seen as part of administration, so a raised road led from the entrance kiosk to the administration building, a curved block carried on a single line of pilotis, facing back to the village of Melsungen, where it had all started. From there, parties had to traverse the long loggia leading from administration to production. Now visitors can be dealt with more immediately, with less disruption to the working life of the building, and the job of entertaining them has become more streamlined, including the ability to offer them lunch in the nearby canteen. In a building devoted to capitalist production, public relations are an essential part of the equation.

Visitors may represent existing and potential customers, or they may be members of staff and of the local community, which to a large degree identifies with what was originally a local family business. They are received in the ground floor entrance hall, at the nearest end of the production building. A permanent exhibition of the history and aims of the company unfolds as the visitors rise up through the various levels, culminating in the visitor balcony overlooking the full length of the production hall and explaining the processes involved as they are viewed. Seminars are held at the midpoint of the exhibition sequence, and visitors return by lift to the entrance hall. The very existence of this programme has probably contributed to the success and growth of the company.

So the building continues in the functionalist tradition in which it was conceived. But what of its place within architecture?

How is a building to be placed within architecture? This can only be done through its own awareness of its place. Here there is one clear reference, and that is to Peter Behrens' AEG Turbine Factory in Berlin, conceived in 1908, a forerunner of the Modern Movement in architecture. It belongs to that initial phase of rapid change that Richard Rogers prefers. The mainly unglazed upper part of the Braun building reads as a sort of pedimental space, as in Behrens, and the segmental vault above has five facets, to Behrens' six, and appears more curved, because it is also curved in plan, as part of its functional job of providing a shelter above the main entrance. The segmental roof was integral to the production building in the original design by Stirling-Wilford. The building is of its own time, particularly in being more horizontal in its proportions, but the likeness is unmistakable.

The Turbine Factory was illustrated in Frampton's *Critical History* (p. 113), where he says:

Far from being a straightforward design in iron and glass… Behren's
Turbine Factory was a conscious work of art, a temple to industrial power. [2]

It is also evident that in relating to a famous forerunner of modernity in architecture, Michael Wilford is referring above all to the idea of modern architecture. He is willing to be compared with a famous example, but one that at its inception was conscious of architecture's aspirations as art, and while Behrens was anxious to promote change, he also wanted to declare its allegiance to a classical tradition. In this Wilford and Schupp have also declared their allegiance to the tradition established by James Stirling, and reflected at Melsungen by many aspects that are also balanced between past and future.[3]

There is a pleasing play of asymmetry in the new front elevation: the doors are forced to the left by the rising ground to the right, and are sheltered by an immediate overhang, while the main roof overhang high above is broadly symmetrical (although actually the middle section is slightly sloped) and emphasised by the large letters B BRAUN. Wilford has added his own mark to the building, but with a characteristic modesty that leaves a lot to Stirling.

Inside the exhibition space the building continues to display a complete unity of form. A certain intricacy of the circulation accompanies the way up, confirming the visitors' sense of adventure. At the upper ground contour, one's view into the intermediate level of the production building is somewhat intimidated by crossed beams above, vaguely reminiscent (to the writer at least) of Wells Cathedral. But the visitor is welcomed by the display of historical pieces, and soothed by the use of strong colour on the rear walls. The stairs, ramps and walls are all conceived within a minimalist style that confirms the purpose of the building as a centre of industrial production.

In this building, Stirling lives on, and this is something for which we can be grateful to Michael Wilford and Manuel Schupp.

London, March 2010, published September 2010.

1. Rogers, Richard, *Architecture: A Modern View*, Thames & Hudson, 1990.
2. Frampton, Kenneth, *Modern Architecture: A Critical History*, Thames & Hudson, 1980
3. Maxwell, Robert, "The Far Side of Modernity", in *Architectural Review*, December 1992.

ACKNOWLEDGEMENTS

I would like to thank the following:

Duncan McCorquodale, my publisher:
for initiating this book,

Kate Trant, of Artifice books on architecture:
for her help and forbearance in furthering the programme.

Michael Wilford, my friend:
for his help and encouragement.

Celia Scott, my partner:
for telling me what to do next.

INDEX

IMAGE CREDITS

Project: *Club for the Peak*, Hong Kong
Zaha Hadid, 1982 © Zaha Hadid, Courtesy
Zaha Hadid Architects

Jewish Museum, Berlin (site model)
Daniel Libeskind, 1993–1995 © Studio Daniel
Libeskind

Villa Dall'Ava
Rem Koolhaas, 1990 © OMA, photographer,
Hans Werlemann (Hectic Pictures)

Project in Seattle
Richard Rogers, 1984
© Richard Rogers Partnership

Apartment Complex, Vienna
Coop Himmelb(l)au, 1983
Photograph © Gerald Zugmann photography

Hongkong and Shanghai bank
Norman Foster

Berlin Free-Zone: Free-space section
Lebbeus Woods, 1990 © Lebbeus Woods

Underground Berlin—Alexanderplatz
Lebbeus Woods, 1988 © Lebbeus Woods

Waterloo International Station, View from outside
Nicholas Grimshaw, 1983 © Grimshaw,
photograph; John Edward Linden

Waterloo International Station, View inside
Nicholas Grimshaw, 1983 © Grimshaw,
photograph; Jo Reid and John Peck

Church with the Light
Tadao Ando, 1989 © Tadao Ando,
photographer Shigeo Anzai

O House
Tadao Ando, 1988 © Tadao Ando,
photographer Mitsuo Matsuoka

Housing at Gallaratese, Milan
Aldo Rossi, 1973
Photograph © Robert Maxwell

Housing at Gallaratese. Detail of the fat columns
Aldo Rossi
Photograph © Robert Maxwell

Fingal County Hall
Bucholz McEvoy Architects, 2001
Photograph © Michael Moran Photography Inc.

Double House in Hampstead
Jonathan Woolf Architects © Jonathan Woolf
Architects, Hélène Binet photographer

House near Bargemon
Edward and Margot Jones, 2004
Photograph © Robert Maxwell

The Peace Palace Library, The Hague
Wilford Schupp Architects, 2008 © Wilford
Schupp, photographer Peter de Ruig, Den
Haag, NL

Lights Red over Black
Mark Rothko © 1998 Kate Rothko Prizel &
Christopher Rothko ARS, NY and DACS,
London

Chief
Franz Kline © ARS, NY and DACS, London
2012

Spiral
Marcel Duchamp
© Succession Marcel Duchamp/ADAGP, Paris
and DACS, London 2012

Enigma of the Day
de Chirico © DACS 2012

Portrait of George Dyer in a Mirror, 1968
Francis Bacon, 1968
Fundación Thyssen-Bornemisza, Madrid
© The Estate of Francis Bacon. All rights
reserved. DACS, London

COLOPHON

© 2012 Artifice books on architecture, the architects and the authors.
All rights reserved.

Artifice books on architecture
10A Acton Street
London
WC1X 9NG

t. +44 (0)207 713 5097
f. +44 (0)207 713 8682
sales@artificebooksonline.com
www.artificebooksonline.com

All opinions expressed within this publication are those of the authors and
not necessarily of the publisher.

Designed by Mónica Oliveira at Artifice books on architecture.
Edited at Artifice books on architecture.

British Library Cataloguing-in-Publication Data.
A CIP record for this book is available from the British Library.

ISBN 978 1 908967 07 7

Artifice books on architecture is an environmentally responsible company.
A Few Years of Writing is printed on sustainably sourced paper.